スピーキングのための
英熟語
English What They Really Use

Matthew D. Kim

IBCパブリッシング

ENGLISH WHAT THEY REALLY USE
By Matthew D. Kim

Copyright ©2015 by Matthew D. Kim
All right reserved

Japanese Language copyright ©2016 IBC PUBLISHING
Japanese translation rights arranged with Humankind Books
through Eric Yang Agency Inc.

はじめに

　以前、数名のニューヨーカーに慣用句（イディオム）とは何かと尋ねたことがあります。驚いたことに、彼らは正確な意味を答えることができませんでした。彼らにとって慣用句とは、あえて定義をする必要がないほど自然な言語であり、文化だからです。

　アメリカ英語は、表現が豊かで変化に富んでいますが、その中でも特にトレンドに敏感なニューヨークに住んでいる人々が使用する英語は、慣用的な表現に満ちています。英語全体で見たときに、慣用句にはなんと10,000を超える表現があり、その中には最近生まれたものもあれば、百年以上にわたって使われてきたものも含まれます。

　慣用句は、カジュアルな場面や会話だけで使われるものではありません。公式な席の会話や、ビジネス用の書類やメールなどの書き言葉にも使用される、ある意味で英語には必須の要素なのです。

　アメリカの人たちは、自分が言いたいことを迅速かつ簡単に、そして分かりやすく伝えるために慣用表現を使用します。これは、話し手の相手への親近感やセンスを引き立てるための最良の手段なのです。

　例えば緊張感が漂うような場での慣用句の使用は、硬い雰囲気を緩和させてくれる効果があります。あれこれと言葉を並べたてて述べるよりも、慣用句を一言使った方がより効果的であるようなこともあります。

　アメリカ英語で自然なコミュニケーションをするために、本書に掲載している多様な表現を身につけることをおススメします。

意味を確認するだけではなく、正しい使い方や話す相手・場所も考慮してください。

　本書『スピーキングのための英熟語』は、著者がニューヨークで、あらゆる人たちとコミュニケーションする中で一つ一つ記録していった、本物のアメリカ英語の慣用表現を集めています。表現やその意味に加え、イラストをあわせて掲載しています。これを見ながら、"使えるシチュエーション"を頭に叩き込みましょう。

　ネイティブのアメリカ人が使う熟語はもっとたくさんあるでしょうが、読者のみなさんの負担にならないように、本書では実際に使用することの多い、必須慣用表現だけ492個を厳選しました。慣用句を集中して勉強したい読者だけではなく、慣用表現を会話相手に楽しく使ってみたいと考えているような方にも利用していただきたいと思います。

　『スピーキングのための英熟語』は、使える英語を学ぼうとする読者のみなさんのコミュニケーションスキルを最大限に向上させてくれるでしょう。

Contents

Day 01 · · · · · · · · · · · · · · · · · · 15
about-face
about time
ace in the hole
act up
after all
a little bird told me
all ears
an arm and a leg
around the clock
as hard as nails
at any rate
at death's door

Day 02 · · · · · · · · · · · · · · · · · · 23
at first sight
at leisure
at odds
at one's doorstep
at the eleventh hour
at this juncture
backseat driver
bad blood
bad mouth
bang up
beat it
beauty sleep

Day 03 · · · · · · · · · · · · · · · · · · 31
beef up
beat one's gums
before long
be hard on
behind one's back
be in a stew
be into something
be my guest!
beyond one's means
big hand
big head
big time

Day 04 · · · · · · · · · · · · · · · · · · 39
bite one's lips
bitter pill
black and blue
black day
black out
blind spot
blow one's mind
blue in the face
bone up
born with a silver spoon in one's mouth
born yesterday
bottle up

Day 05 · · · · · · · · · · · · · · · · · · 47
bottom line
boys will be boys
brainwash
bread and butter
break one's neck
break the ice
break the record
break through
bring around
bring home the bacon
bug in one's ear
bullshit

Day 06 · · · · · · · · · · · · · · · · · · 55
burn one's fingers
burn the midnight oil
burst into
burst into tears
buy for a song
by a long shot
by and large
by chance
by means of
B.Y.O.B
by oneself
by word of mouth

5

Contents

Day 07 63
- call it a day
- call off
- call on
- call out
- can of worms
- carry a tune
- carry out
- catch it
- catch on
- catch one's eye
- catch some rays
- chain-smoke

Day 08 71
- change hands
- change one's tune
- cheapskate
- chew the fat
- chime in
- chip off the old block
- clip one's wings
- closed book
- cold shoulder
- cold snap
- collect dust
- come about

Day 09 79
- come again
- come alive
- come by
- come out in the open
- come out with
- come through for
- come to light
- come up with
- common ground
- common touch
- compare notes
- cool as a cucumber

Day 10 87
- cool customer
- coop up
- cop out
- copy cat
- couch potato
- couldn't care less
- count on
- cover up
- cozy up
- crack a book
- crack a joke
- crack the whip

Day 11 95
- not all cracked up to be
- creep up on
- crocodile tears
- crop up
- cross one's path
- cross swords
- cry on one's shoulder
- cut a class
- cut a deal
- cut corners
- cut one's throat
- cut the mustard

Day 12 103
- cut up
- dare say
- dark horse
- dash light
- day by day
- day in and day out
- day of reckoning
- days are numbered
- dead duck
- dead to the world
- dear me
- diamond in the rough

Day 13 111

die on the vine
dirt cheap
dish the dirt
do a double take
do away with
doggy bag
doll up
do or die
double up
down and out
draw a blank
drift off

Day 14 119

drink down
drink like a fish
drive one crazy
dropout
drown out
duck out
dying to
ear to the ground
easygoing
easy come, easy go
eat like a bird
eat like a horse

Day 15 127

every cloud has a silver lining
eyes pop out
fair-weather friend
fall flat
fall guy
far cry
fed up
feel down
feel for someone
feet of clay
filthy rich
first come, first served

Day 16 135

fish out of water
flesh and blood
flush it
flying high
fly in the ointment
fly the coop
food for thought
fool around
foot in the door
for all I know
for days on end
for dear life

Day 17 143

fork over
for sure
for the better
freak out
free rein
from scratch
from the heart
from time to time
fuddy-duddy
full-bodied
full-fledged
game is up

Day 18 151

gee whiz
get across
get a grip on
get a kick out of
get a rise out of
get back at
get behind
get by
get going
get off one's back
get on one's case
get real

Contents

Day 19 159
- get the eye
- get the sack
- get under one's skin
- get up on the wrong side of the bed
- get with it
- give it to one straight
- give no quarter
- give up the ghost
- go after
- go astray
- gobble up
- go Dutch

Day 20 167
- go-getter
- going on
- good egg
- good-for-nothing
- goof off
- go steady
- go straight
- go wrong
- green with envy
- grin and bear it
- gung-ho
- had better

Day 21 175
- hand over fist
- hands down
- hangover
- happy camper
- hardheaded
- hard line
- have an eye for
- have got to
- have in mind
- have it coming
- have one's cake and eat it too
- have the last laugh

Day 22 183
- hell and high water
- hem and haw
- hit-and-run
- hit a nerve
- hit home
- hit it off
- hit the ceiling
- hit the hay
- hit the road
- honeymoon is over
- hooked on
- horse sense

Day 23 191
- hot air
- hot potato
- I couldn't agree with you more
- ill at ease
- in a pinch
- in charge of
- in kind
- in one's shoes
- ins and outs
- in the cards
- in the clouds
- in the limelight

Day 24 199
- in the red
- in the same boat
- into thin air
- in tune
- in vain
- jawbreaker
- jump to a conclusion
- just in case
- keel over
- keen about
- keep after
- keep an eye on

Day 25 207

keep one's nose clean
keep the ball rolling
keep up with the Joneses
keyed up
kick the bucket
kick up one's heels
kill time
knock about
knock oneself out
know where one stands
landslide
last but not least

Day 26 215

laundry list
lay a finger on
lay away
lead off
lean on
leave no stone unturned
let down
let bygones be bygones
let go of
let one's hair down
let the cat out of the bag
level playing field

Day 27 223

life and limb
light up
like two peas in a pod
live from hand to mouth
live it up
living end
look out
lose one's heart
lose touch
big mouth
mad about
main squeeze

Day 28 231

make a mountain out of a molehill
make-believe
make ends meet
make eyes at
make hay while the sun shines
make neither head nor tail of
make one's head spin
make one's mark
make one's mouth water
make up one's mind
man in the street
matter of course

Day 29 239

meet up with
mend one's ways
mess around
monkey on one's back
more the merrier
morning after
move heaven and earth
mum is the word
music to one's ears
my lips are sealed
nail down
namedropper

Day 30 247

no doubt
no sweat
nutty as a fruitcake
oddball
off the hook
off the record
off the top of one's head
once and for all
once in a blue moon
on cloud nine
on easy street
one on the city

9

Contents

Day 31 255
- on one's knees
- on purpose
- on the dot
- on the double
- on the homestretch
- on the house
- on the market
- on the same page with
- on the tip of one's tongue
- out of place
- out of this world
- out of whack

Day 32 263
- pain in the ass
- palm off
- pass away
- pay the piper
- pay through the nose
- pick-me-up
- pick the brains of
- piece of cake
- piss off
- play on
- play one's cards right
- pour out

Day 33 271
- promise the moon
- pull one's leg
- pull strings
- pushover
- put up with
- put words into one's mouth
- put money where your mouth is
- quite the thing
- rain check
- read the riot act
- right on
- ring a bell

Day 34 279
- rip-off
- rob the cradle
- roller coaster ride
- root for
- rule out
- run off
- run over
- run that by me again
- save the day
- say a mouthful
- scratch the surface
- screw up

Day 35 287
- second thought
- second wind
- see things
- set out
- set the world on fire
- show off
- sick and tired
- sink in
- sleep a wink
- sleep like a dog
- sleep on
- smell a rat

Day 36 295
- so far, so good
- speak of the devil and he appears
- split hairs
- spring chicken
- stab in the back
- stand in for
- steal the show
- stick-in-the-mud
- stuck on
- sure thing
- swallow one's words
- take advantage of

Day 37 303

- take a stand
- take back
- take it on the chin
- taken aback
- take the edge off
- talk back
- taper down
- tell on
- the creeps
- the score
- think aloud
- think better of

Day 38 311

- think over
- through the grapevine
- through thick and thin
- throw in the towel
- tickle pink
- tie the knot
- tighten one's belt
- time and again
- tip the scales
- to a man
- to a turn
- to boot

Day 39 319

- top-drawer
- to speak of
- to this day
- trial and error
- try one's hand
- turn the tide
- twiddle one's thumbs
- two-time
- under a cloud
- under one's breath
- under one's wing
- under the sun

Day 40 327

- up-and-coming
- ups and downs
- uptight
- use up
- verbal diarrhea
- wade in
- wait up
- walk in the park
- warm up
- waste one's breath
- way to go
- weasel word

Day 41 335

- whipping boy
- white lie
- wise up to
- word for word
- world is one's oyster
- wrapped up in
- write home about
- X-rated
- yes-man
- you bet
- your guess is as good as mine
- zonk out

スピーキングのための
英熟語
English What They Really Use

Matthew D. Kim

01 about-face
名 (180度の)方針転換

The high school did an about-face over hairstyle restrictions.
その高校は髪型の制限について180度の方針転換をした。

▶▶ もとは軍の号令で、「回れ右」の意味。do an about-face として使う。

02 about time
名 句 もう〜してもいい頃

It's about time you got up, Mark.
もう起きてもいい頃よ、マーク。

It's about time Ricky should have got here.
リッキーがもうここに着いていてもいい頃だ。

▶▶ It's about time. で「そろそろ時間だよ」の意味でよく使う表現。

03 ace in the hole
名 句 とっておきの切り札

The lawyer's ace in the hole was a secret witness who saw the accident.
弁護士のとっておきの切り札は、事故を目撃した秘密の証人だった。

▶▶ play one's ace で、「奥の手を使う」という表現もある。

Let's Review

01 The high school did an _____ over hairstyle restrictions.

その高校は髪型の制限について180度の方針転換をした。

02 It's _____ you got up, Mark.

もう起きてもいい頃よ、マーク。

03 The lawyer's _____ was a secret witness who saw the accident.

弁護士のとっておきの切り札は、事故を目撃した秘密の証人だった。

解答 **01** about-face **02** about time **03** ace in the hole

DAY 01

04 act up
動 インフォーマル 騒ぐ、行儀よくしない

The dog acted up as the postman came to the door.
郵便配達員が戸口に来ると犬が騒いだ。

▶▶ くだけた感じで、子どもがいたずらをしてはしゃぎ回る、というような時にも使う。

05 after all
副 句 結局

Brian thought he couldn't go to the party because he had too much homework, but he went after all.
ブライアンは宿題が多すぎてパーティーに行けないと思っていたが、結局行った。

▶▶ そうではないと思っていたけれど、やっぱりというニュアンスがある。通例は文尾に使われる。

06 a little bird told me
うわさを聞いた、ある人から聞いた

A little bird told me your sister was having big problems.
妹さんが大変な問題を抱えているといううわさを聞きました。

▶▶ 〈話〉that 節が続く。話の出所を曖昧にしたいときに使う。

Let's Review

04 The dog _____ as the postman came to the door.

郵便配達員が戸口に来ると犬が騒いだ。

05 Brian thought he couldn't go to the party because he had too much homework, but he went _____.

ブライアンは宿題が多すぎてパーティーに行けないと思っていたが、結局行った。

06 _____ your sister was having big problems.

妹さんが大変な問題を抱えているといううわさを聞きました。

解答 **04** acted up　**05** after all　**06** A little bird told me

all ears
形 句 耳を傾ける、熱心に聞く

Tell me what you think about Mark. I'm all ears.

マークをどう思っているか私に教えて。耳を傾けているから。

▶▶ I'm all ears. で「ちゃんと聞いてるよ」、I'm listening. にも近い。

an arm and a leg
名 多額の金、法外な金

Vacations don't have to cost an arm and a leg. We'll show you how to save and still have fun!

休暇に多額の金を費やす必要はありません。節約しながら楽しむ方法をお教えしましょう！

▶▶ cost an arm and leg で「大金がかかった」、charge an arm and leg for で「法外な値段をつける」となる。

around the clock
副 句 24時間ぶっ通しで、一日中

Brian studied around the clock for his math exam.

ブライアンは数学の試験のために24時間ぶっ通しで勉強した。

▶▶ 時計の針がぐるっと回るから、「休みなく一日中」の意味になると覚えるとよい。

Let's Review

07 Tell me what you think about Mark. I'm _____.

マークをどう思っているか私に教えて。耳を傾けているから。

08 Vacations don't have to cost _____. We'll show you how to save and still have fun!

休暇に多額の金を費やす必要はありません。節約しながら楽しむ方法をお教えしましょう！

09 Brian studied _____ for his math exam.

ブライアンは数学の試験のために24時間ぶっ通しで勉強した。

解答 **07** all ears **08** an arm and a leg **09** around the clock

⑩ as hard as nails
[副句] 無慈悲な、無慈悲な

Eva is as hard as nails. Although she is a millionaire, she doesn't help her less fortunate relatives.
エヴァは無慈悲だ。大金持ちだけど、それほど恵まれていない親戚を助けない。

▶▶ 他の人に何の感情も同情も感じないほどタフな人、または身体が強健という意味もある。

⑪ at any rate
[副句] とにかく、それにしても

At any rate, Mark is a great Account Executive.
とにかく、マークは優秀な顧客担当者だ。

▶▶ exact, verbatim と同義。

⑫ at death's door
[形 副 句] 瀕死で、重体で

My iPhone is at death's door. New one is ordered and will hopefully arrive tomorrow.
僕のiPhoneは瀕死だ。新しいのを注文したけど、明日来るといいな。

▶▶ 病気の人や動物にも使える。The family dog was at death's door for three days. といえば、「飼い犬がもう3日も死にそうな状態だ」ということ。

Let's Review

10 Eva is _____. Although she is a millionaire, she doesn't help her less fortunate relatives.

エヴァは無慈悲だ。大金持ちだけど、それほど恵まれていない親戚を助けない。

11 _____, Mark is a great Account Executive.

とにかく、マークは優秀な顧客担当者だ。

12 My iPhone is _____. New one is ordered and will hopefully arrive tomorrow.

僕のiPhoneは瀕死だ。新しいのを注文したけど、明日来るといいな。

解答 **10** as hard as nails **11** At any rate **12** at death's door

DAY 02

01 at first sight
形 一目で

Mark met Julia at a party, and it was a love at first sight.
マークはパーティーでジュリアに会い、一目で恋に落ちた。

▶▶ At first sight I thought the test was easy. のように使えば、「一見したところ〜」の意味になる。

---

02 at leisure
形 副 句 時間の余裕があって、暇で

Come and visit us some evening when you're at leisure.
時間の余裕がある晩にでも遊びに来てください。

▶▶ at one'e leisure、at one's convenience も同義。leisure には、働いてない時、リラックスしている時の意味がある。

---

03 at odds
副 句 もめて、対立して

Eva and Mark are always at odds about little things.
エヴァとマークはいつもちょっとしたことでもめる。

▶▶ 人と争う場合は、「with + 人」何かについて争うという場合は、「over + 事」になる。

Let's Review

01 Mark met Julia at a party, and it was a love _____.

マークはパーティーでジュリアに会い、一目で恋に落ちた。

02 Come and visit us some evening when you're _____.

時間の余裕がある晩にでも遊びに来てください。

03 Eva and Mark are always _____ about little things.

エヴァとマークはいつもちょっとしたことでもめる。

解答 **01** at first sight **02** at leisure **03** at odds

DAY 02

at one's doorstep
副句 すぐ近くに、目の前に

Alice enjoys the convenience because there's a subway station right at her doorstep.
地下鉄の駅がすぐ近くにあるので、アリスは便利な生活をしている。

▶▶ at death's doorstep で「瀕死の状態」。

at the eleventh hour
副句 ぎりぎりに、間際に

Brian always turned his report in at the eleventh hour.
ブライアンはいつもぎりぎりにレポートを提出した。

Alice got a concert ticket at the eleventh hour.
アリスはコンサートのチケットをぎりぎりで入手した。

▶▶ 11時は、Just before the last clock hour, 12. なので、本当にぎりぎりなこと。

at this juncture
副句 現在のところ、今ここで

At this juncture, the designer is still uncertain as to how to proceed.
今ここで、デザイナーはどう進めるべきかまだわかっていない。

▶▶ juncture は「(重大な) 時点」の意味がある。

Let's Review

04 Alice enjoys the convenience because there's a subway station right _____.

地下鉄の駅がすぐ近くにあるので、アリスは便利な生活をしている。

05 Brian always turned his report in _____.

ブライアンはいつもぎりぎりにレポートを提出した。

06 _____, the designer is still uncertain as to how to proceed.

今ここで、デザイナーはどう進めるべきかまだわかっていない。

解答 **04** at her doorstep　**05** at the eleventh hour　**06** At this juncture

backseat driver
 名 インフォーマル 余計な口出しをする人、お節介焼き

Stop being a backseat driver! I am sick and tired of it!

余計な口出しをするのはやめてくれ！　もううんざりだ！

▶▶ 必ずしも後部座席に座ってなくても、運転もしないのに、あれこれと指示出しする人は backseat driver。

---

bad blood
 名 インフォーマル わだかまり、不仲

There's a lot of bad blood between Eva and Mark. I bet they'll never talk to each other again.

エヴァとマークはずいぶんわだかまりがある。お互いに口を利くことは二度とないだろうね。

▶▶ 2人の間に、非常に気まずい空気がながれていること。

---

bad mouth
 動 スラング 悪口を言う、中傷する

I don't think it is ever a good idea to bad mouth the boss or anyone else you work with.

上司や同僚の悪口を言うのは良いこととは思わないね。

▶▶ 過去形は bad-mouthed、現在分詞は bad-mouthing など、動詞の活用形でも使う。三人称は bad-mouths。

Let's Review

07 Stop being a _____ ! I am sick and tired of it!

余計な口出しをするのはやめてくれ！もううんざりだ！

08 There's a lot of _____ between Eva and Mark. I bet they'll never talk to each other again.

エヴァとマークはずいぶんわだかまりがある。お互いに口を利くことは二度とないだろうね。

09 I don't think it is ever a good idea to _____ the boss or anyone else you work with.

上司や同僚の悪口を言うのは良いこととは思わないね。

解答 **07** backseat driver **08** bad blood **09** bad mouth

DAY 02

10 bang up
形 インフォーマル 素晴らしい、最高の

In fact, Mark and Brian have done a bang up job of selling the new product.

実際、マークとブライアンは新製品の販売に当たり素晴らしい仕事をした。

▶▶ bang up は、「壊す、傷つける」の意味にもなるので要注意。

---

11 beat it
動 スラング ❶逃げる

When Mark heard the crash he beat it as fast as he could.

マークは破壊音を聞くと、できるだけ速く逃げた。

❷出ていく

Beat it, Alice. We don't want you to be with us.

出ていけよ、アリス。君にいてほしくないんだ。

▶▶ マイケル・ジャクソンの歌でもおなじみの表現。Go on, beat it! としてよく使う。

---

12 beauty sleep
名 美容のための睡眠

Julia took her beauty sleep before the party.

ジュリアはパーティーの前に美容のための睡眠をとった。

▶▶ sleeping beauty は、眠れる美女。beatuty sleep で、美しく健康になるための睡眠となる。

Let's Review

10 In fact, Mark and Brian have done a _____ job of selling the new product.

実際、マークとブライアンは新製品の販売に当たり素晴らしい仕事をした。

11 When Mark heard the crash he _____ as fast as he could.

マークは破壊音を聞くと、できるだけ速く逃げた。

12 Julia took her _____ before the party.

ジュリアはパーティーの前に美容のための睡眠をとった。

解答 **10** bang up **11** beat it **12** beauty sleep

01 **beef up**

動 インフォーマル (組織、制度などを)補強する、増強する

President Obama wants to beef up border security.

オバマ大統領は国境警備を補強したいと望んでいる。

▶▶ Let's beef this music up with more on piano. とすれば「ピアノをもっと効かせて、楽曲を良くしよう」の意味になる。

02 **beat one's gums**

動 句 スラング 無駄話をする、だらだら話す

Mark as usual is beating his gums for nothing.

マークはいつも通りどうでもいい無駄話をしている。

Quit beating your gums and do something constructive while you are at work.

仕事中に無駄話をするのはやめて、建設的なことをしなさい。

▶▶ ここでのgum(s)は歯ぐき、歯肉のこと。

03 **before long**

副 句 まもなく、すぐに

It will be dark before long.

まもなく暗くなるだろう。

They might be forgotten before long.

まもなく彼らは忘れられるかもしれない。

▶▶ soonと同様に使う。Billy will be grown-up before long (=soon).

Let's Review

01 President Obama wants to _____ border security.

オバマ大統領は国境警備を補強したいと望んでいる。

02 Quit _____ and do something constructive while you are at work.

仕事中に無駄話をするのはやめて、建設的なことをしなさい。

03 They might be forgotten _____.

まもなく彼らは忘れられるかもしれない。

解答 **01** beef up　**02** beating your gums　**03** before long

DAY 03

 ## be hard on
動 句 つらく当たる、責める

Mark is so hard on a new employee for just a minor mistake.

マークは、小さなミスをしたからといって新人をひどく責める。

▶▶ Don't be too hard on me. で「お手柔らかに」。日常的によく使われる表現。

 ## behind one's back
副 句 (人の)いない時に、背後で、(人に)内緒で

Say it to his face, not behind his back.

彼のいない時ではなく、面と向かって言いなさい。

They whispered behind Julia's back.

彼らはジュリアの背後で耳打ちした。

▶▶ 反対の「面と向かって」は to one's face。

 ## be in a stew
動 句 イライラしている、思い悩む

Brian has been in a stew ever since he got the word that Alice was going to marry his worst enemy.

ブライアンは、アリスが自分の最大の敵と結婚すると耳にして以来ずっとイライラしている。

▶▶ in the soup なら「困って、苦境にあって」となる。

Let's Review

04 Mark _____ a new employee for just a minor mistake.

マークは、小さなミスをしたからといって新人をひどく責める。

05 They whispered _____.

彼らはジュリアの背後で耳打ちした。

06 Brian has _____ ever since he got the word that Alice was going to marry his worst enemy.

ブライアンは、アリスが自分の最大の敵と結婚すると耳にして以来ずっとイライラしている。

解答 **04** is so hard on　**05** behind Julia's back　**06** been in a stew

DAY 03

07 **be into something**
動 句 インフォーマル ～に熱中している

Did you know that Julia is seriously into learning guitar?
ジュリアがギターの演奏を覚えようとひどく熱中してること、知ってた？

▶▶ 何かに「ハマる」のニュアンスで使ってみよう。

---

08 **be my guest!**
動 句 どうぞご自由に（お使いください）、いいですとも

"Can I borrow that pencil?" Mark asked Julia. "Be my guest!" Julia answered.
「そのえんぴつを借りていい？」とマークはジュリアにたずねた。「どうぞご自由に！」とジュリアは答えた。

▶▶ 「私のお客さんになって」ということで、「遠慮なくどうぞ～してください」の意味。

---

09 **beyond one's means**
形 句 （値段が高くて）手が届かない、収入の範囲を超えて

Unfortunately, The Mercedes-Benz is beyond my means right now.
残念だけど、メルセデス・ベンツは、今はぼくの手に届かない。

▶▶ means には、「方法」の他に、「資産、富」の意味がある。

Let's Review

07 Did you know that Julia _____ guitar?

ジュリアがギターの演奏を覚えようとひどく熱中してること、知ってた？

08 "Can I borrow that pencil?" Mark asked Julia. "_____" Julia answered.

「そのえんぴつを借りていい？」とマークはジュリアにたずねた。「どうぞご自由に！」とジュリアは答えた。

09 Unfortunately, The Mercedes-Benz is _____ right now.

残念だけど、メルセデス・ベンツは、今はぼくの手に届かない。

解答 **07** is seriously into learning **08** Be my guest! **09** beyond my means

10 big hand
名 大喝采、盛大な拍手

When DOK2 finished rapping 'Handz Up', they got a very big hand.

DOK2 がラップの「ハンズアップ」を歌い終えると、大喝采を得た。

▶▶ get、have、give などの動詞とともに使われることが多い。

---

11 big head
名 インフォーマル 自負心、自尊心

When Mark was promoted as the director of the company, it gave him a big head.

マークは会社の重役に昇進して、自負心が芽生えた。

▶▶ 形容詞で使う場合は、big-headed となる。

---

12 big time
名 インフォーマル ❶とても楽しい時、ゆかいなひと時

Mark and Julia had a big time at the club last night.

マークとジュリアは昨晩クラブでとても楽しい時を過ごした。

❷一流、大物

Many young actors get to Hollywood, but only a few of them reach the big time.

多くの若い俳優がハリウッドにやって来るが、一流になるのはほんの一握りだ。

▶▶ 副詞として使う場合は「極めて」や「ひどく」という意味になる。
He messed up big time!「彼はひどい失敗をした！」

Let's Review

10 When DOK2 finished rapping 'Handz Up', they got a very _____.

DOK2 がラップの「ハンズアップ」を歌い終えると、大喝采を得た。

11 When Mark was promoted as the director of the company, it gave him a _____.

マークは会社の重役に昇進して、自負心が芽生えた。

12 Mark and Julia had a _____ at the club last night.

マークとジュリアは昨晩クラブでとても楽しい時を過ごした。

解答　**10** big hand　**11** big head　**12** big time

01 bite one's lips
動句 くやしい思いをする、唇をかむ

I had to bite my lips when I heard my boss gave the wrong orders.

上司が間違った指示をしたと聞いて、私はくやしい思いをした。

▶▶ I really wanted to laugh — I had to bite my lip. のように、笑いをかみ殺したいときにも使える。

02 bitter pill
名 つらいもの、苦い薬

The truth is a bitter pill to swallow. Except for when it's sweet.

真実は受け入れ難くつらいものだ。よい話の時を除いて。

▶▶ pill は「錠剤」の意味。薬は苦くても、飲む（受け入れる）しかない。

03 black and blue
形 青黒くなっている、痛そうな

Mark was black and blue after he fell off the chair.

マークはイスから落ちたあと、青黒いあざができた。

Alice ran off with tears in her eyes. Her arm was black and blue.

アリスは目に涙を浮かべて走り去った。彼女の腕はあざで痛々しかった。

▶▶ 「自分の目の色は黒です」のつもりで I have black eyes. と言うと「目のまわりにあざがある」という意味になってしまうので注意。

Let's Review

01 I had to _____ when I heard my boss gave the wrong orders.

上司が間違った指示をしたと聞いて、私はくやしい思いをした。

02 The truth is a _____ to swallow. Except for when it's sweet.

真実は受け入れ難くつらいものだ。よい話の時を除いて。

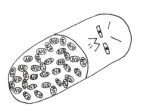

03 Mark was _____ after he fell off the chair.

マークはイスから落ちたあと、青黒いあざができた。

解答 **01** bite my lips **02** bitter pill **03** black and blue

DAY 04

04 black day
名 暗黒の日

It was a black day for this area when the local steel factory closed down.
鉄工場が閉鎖された時が、この地域にとっての暗黒の日だった。

▶▶「最悪の日」「陰うつな日」の意味で、よく聞く表現。

---

05 black out
動 ❶真っ暗になる、止まる

My screen just blacked out. 僕の画面が、たったいま真っ暗になった。

❷意識を失う

It had been a hard and tiring day, and Alice suddenly blacked out.
つらく、疲れた一日だった、そしてアリスは突然意識を失った。

▶▶「人が気を失う」は他に、pass out、become unconscious という言い方もある。

---

06 blind spot
名 ❶盲点、不得手な分野

Why does every human being have a blind spot and how to find mine?
なぜ、あらゆる人に不得手な分野があるのだろうか、そして自分のそういう点は、どのようにしたら見つけられるのか？

❷死角

One ignored my right turn signal and came up from my blind spot. 誰かが僕の右折合図を無視して、死角から現れてきた。

▶▶ 同義語は blind side だが、動詞 blindside になると「不意打ちを食らわす」の意味になる。

Let's Review

04 It was a _____ for this area when the local steel factory closed down.

鉄工場が閉鎖された時が、この地域にとっての暗黒の日だった。

05 My screen just _____.

僕の画面が、たったいま真っ暗になった。

06 Why does every human being have a _____ and how to find mine?

なぜ、あらゆる人に不得手な分野があるのだろうか、そして自分のそういう点は、どのようにしたら見つけられるのか？

解答 **04** black day   **05** blacked out   **06** blind spot

DAY 04

blow one's mind
動 句 スラング インフォーマル うっとりさせる

The music Julia was playing really blew my mind.
ジュリアが演奏していた音楽に、ほんとうにうっとりした。

▶▶ 麻薬などが（人に）陶酔感や恍惚感を覚えさせる、という意味でも使う。She blew her mind on drugs.

blue in the face
形 句 インフォーマル 疲れきって口もきけない

Mark argued with Eva until he was blue in the face.
マークは、疲れきって口もきけなくなるまでエヴァと論争した。

▶▶ (until you are) blue in the face の形で使うことが多い。

bone up
動 インフォーマル 詰め込み勉強する、磨きをかける

Brian was boning up for a final examination.
ブライアンは最終試験に備えて詰め込みで勉強していた。

I'm boning up on my Taekwondo skills now.
僕はいま、テコンドーの技に磨きをかけているところだ。

▶▶ 19世紀半ば、Henry George Bohn という人の書いたテキストで学生が必死に勉強したことが由来とされるが、定かではない。

Let's Review

07 The music Julia was playing really _____.

ジュリアが演奏していた音楽に、ほんとうにうっとりした。

08 Mark argued with Eva until he was _____.

マークは、疲れきって口もきけなくなるまでエヴァと論争した。

09 Brian was _____ for a final examination.

ブライアンは最終試験に備えて詰め込みで勉強していた。

解答 **07** blew my mind **08** blue in the face **09** boning up

DAY 04

10 born with a silver spoon in one's mouth
形 句　裕福な家に生まれる

I wasn't born with a silver spoon in my mouth, but I put one in later.

僕は裕福な家に生まれたわけじゃないけれど、後からそうなった。

▶▶ 裕福な家では銀のスプーンで子どもに食べさせていたことが由来とされ、生まれついての金持ちの意となる。

11 born yesterday
形 句　何も知らない、未経験の

I hate when dudes treat me like I was born yesterday and insult my intelligence.

彼らが僕のことを何も知らないかのように扱い、僕の知性を無視するのがほんとうにいやだ。

▶▶ 否定形で、I wasn't born yesteday. とすれば、「バカにするな！」となる。

12 bottle up
動 句　抑える、隠す

There was no understanding person to talk to, so Mark bottled up his unhappy feeling.

話して理解してくれる人がひとりもいなかったので、マークはつらい気持ちを隠した。

▶▶ 「瓶詰めにする」ように感情を押し殺す、抑えると覚えよう。

Let's Review

10 I wasn't _____, but I put one in later.

僕は裕福な家に生まれたわけじゃないけれど、後からそうなった。

11 I hate when dudes treat me like I was _____ and insult my intelligence.

彼らが僕のことを何も知らないかのように扱い、僕の知性を無視するのがほんとうにいやだ。

12 There was no understanding person to talk to, so Mark _____ his unhappy feeling.

話して理解してくれる人がひとりもいなかったので、マークはつらい気持ちを隠した。

解答 **10** born with a silver spoon in my mouth **11** born yesterday **12** bottled up

DAY 05

01 bottom line
名 インフォーマル 最終収益、結論

I hate when people give me too much information. What is the bottom line?

人があまりに多くのことを知らせてくるのが嫌いだ。結論は何だ？

▶▶ 元々は、決算書などの一番下の欄に最終的な収益が記されていたことから、「主要なこと、肝心なこと」の意味になる。

02 boys will be boys
男の子なんてそんなものだ

Eva said "I am so tired of watching basketball, but oh well boys will be boys I guess."

エヴァは、「野球を見るのにはほんとうに飽き飽きしたけれど、仕方ないか、男の子なんてそんなものだもの」と言った。

▶▶ 男の子だけでなく男性にも使われる。「男の子(男性)とはそういうものだから、仕方ない(あきらめなさい)」のニュアンス。

03 brainwash
動 句 ～を洗脳する、説得して～させる

I've successfully brainwashed people into telling me I'm pretty at least once every 10 minutes.

私は人々を説得して、少なくとも10分ごとに、私に対して可愛いと言わせることに成功した。

▶▶ 「政治・宗教的に洗脳する」の意味でも使う。名詞形は brainwashing。

Let's Review

01 I hate when people give me too much information. What is the _____?

人があまりに多くのことを知らせてくるのが嫌いだ。結論は何だ？

02 Eva said "I am so tired of watching basketball, but oh well _____ I guess."

エヴァは、「野球を見るのにはほんとうに飽き飽きしたけれど、仕方ないか、男の子なんてそんなものだもの」と言った。

03 I've successfully _____ people into telling me I'm pretty at least once every 10 minutes.

私は人々を説得して、少なくとも10分ごとに、私に対して可愛いと言わせることに成功した。

解答 **01** bottom line **02** boys will be boys **03** brainwashed

DAY 05

bread and butter
名 句 生計の手段

Julia earned her bread and butter as a journalist, but added a little jam by working with a band on the weekends.

ジュリアはジャーナリストを生計の手段としていたが、週末にバンドと一緒に働くことで、それに少しプラスしていた。

▶▶ 西欧ではバターを塗ったパンは無くてはならないもの。そこから派生して、生計の手段や生活の糧の意味となった。

break one's neck
動 句 スラング 首の骨を折る、がんばる

Brian nearly broke his neck while learning to water-ski.

ブライアンは水上スキーを習っているとき、もう少しで首の骨を折るところだった。

▶▶ I broke my neck to get here on time.「がんばって時間に間に合うようここに来た」

break the ice
動 句 インフォーマル 緊張をほぐす、話の口火を切る

To break the ice, Mark spoke of his interest in Hip Hop music, and they soon had a conversation going.

話の口火を切るために、マークがヒップホップへの興味について語ると、まもなく会話がはじまった。

▶▶ その場を和ませるときに使う。A nice smile does a lot to break the ice.「その場を和やかにするには、素敵な笑顔が一番だ」

Let's Review

04 Julia earned her _____ as a journalist, but added a little jam by working with a band on the weekends.

ジュリアはジャーナリストを生計の手段としていたが、週末にバンドと一緒に働くことで、それに少しプラスしていた。

05 Brian nearly _____ while learning to water-ski.

ブライアンは水上スキーを習っているとき、もう少しで首の骨を折るところだった。

06 To _____, Mark spoke of his interest in Hip Hop music, and they soon had a conversation going.

話の口火を切るために、マークがヒップホップへの興味について語ると、まもなく会話がはじまった。

解答　04 bread and butter　05 broke his neck　06 break the ice

DAY 05

break the record
動 句 世界記録を破る

Meanwhile the team was trying to break the record for most technical fouls in the playoffs.

その間にチームは、プレーオフにおけるテクニカル・ファウル最多の世界記録を破ろうとしていた。

▶▶ break の代わりに beat, better, cut, shatter, smash と置き換えられる。

---

break through
動 突破する

Tips to break through barriers.

障壁を突破するためのヒントだよ。

▶▶ もともと物理的な障壁を打ち破る意味だったのが、16 世紀後半ごろから抽象的な意味でも使われるようになった。

---

bring around
動 インフォーマル ❶回復させる

Mark was quite ill, but good nursing brought him around.

マークは非常に具合が悪かったが、適切な看護で快方に向かった。

❷（自説などへ）引き入れる

Mark brought Eva around to his way of thinking.

マークは、エヴァを自分の考え方に引き入れた。

▶▶ ❷の「引き入れる」は bring someone around to という形で使われる。

Let's Review

07 Meanwhile the team was trying to _____ for most technical fouls in the playoffs.

その間にチームは、プレーオフにおけるテクニカル・ファウル最多の世界記録を破ろうとしていた。

08 Tips to _____ barriers.

障壁を突破するためのヒントだよ。

09 Mark was quite ill, but good nursing _____.

マークは非常に具合が悪かったが、適切な看護で快方に向かった。

解答 **07** break the record **08** break through **09** brought him around

DAY 05

⑩ bring home the bacon
動句 **インフォーマル** 生活に必要な金を稼ぐ、成功する

Brad and Angelina bring home the bacon.
ブラッドとアンジェリーナは、生活に必要な金を稼いでいる。

▶▶ 昔、baconは貴重だったことから。save one's baconで、「命を救う」という言い方もある。

⑪ bug in one's ear
名句 **インフォーマル** ～のことをちょっと人の耳に入れる

Okay, I'll put a bug in Mark's ear. I hope you two are going well.
オーケー、僕がマークにちょっと耳打ちするよ。君たち2人がうまくいくといいね。

▶▶ これから起きる何かについてのヒントや提案などを与えること。

⑫ bullshit
名卑 **インフォーマル** ふざけた、くだらない

I'm getting sick of your bullshit attitude.
僕は君のふざけた態度にうんざりしかけている。

▶▶ 相手に強く反対したり、強く批判するときにも使うことから、使い方には十分注意を。

Let's Review

10 Brad and Angelina
_____.

ブラッドとアンジェリーナは、生活に必要な金を稼いでいる。

11 Okay, I'll put a _____. I hope you two are going well.

オーケー、僕がマークにちょっと耳打ちするよ。君たち2人がうまくいくといいね。

12 I'm getting sick of your _____ attitude.

僕は君のふざけた態度にうんざりしかけている。

解答 **10** bring home the bacon **11** bug in Mark's ear **12** bullshit

DAY 06

01 burn one's fingers
名句 インフォーマル 痛い目にあう

Eva can't be told. She has to burn her fingers to learn.
エヴァに分からせることはできない。彼女は痛い目にあって覚える必要がある。

▶▶ Many investors burned their fingers on those stocks.「あの株のせいで、多くの投資家が痛い目にあった」のように、お金を失うという痛い目にあうことに使う。

02 burn the midnight oil
動句 (勉強や仕事で)夜ふかしする

Such a stressful day. At first I had to burn the midnight oil.
なんてストレスいっぱいの日なんだ。まずは、夜ふかししなきゃならなかった。

▶▶ 本来は「夜遅くまで勉強する」の意味で使うことが多かったが、今では勉強以外で仕事にも使える。

03 burst into
動句 乱入する、なだれ込む

What would you do if a bunch of monkeys burst into the room this second? Protect all valuable items.
もしサルの群れがこの瞬間、乱入してきたらどうする? 大事なものをすべて守れ。

▶▶ The car burst into flames. といえば、車からあっという間に火の手が上がったことを意味する。

Let's Review

01 Eva can't be told. She has to _____ to learn.

エヴァに分からせることはできない。彼女は痛い目にあって覚える必要がある。

02 Such a stressful day. At first I had to _____.

なんてストレスいっぱいの日なんだ。まずは、夜ふかししなきゃならなかった。

03 What would you do if a bunch of monkeys _____ the room this second? Protect all valuable items.

もしサルの群れがこの瞬間、乱入してきたらどうする？ 大事なものをすべて守れ。

解答 **01** burn her fingers **02** burn the midnight oil **03** burst into

DAY 06

burst into tears
動 句 急に泣き出す

I keep replaying this song. And every time I listen to it, I burst into tears.

僕はこの歌をリプレイし続けている。そしてこの曲を聞くと毎回、急に涙があふれてくるんだ。

▶▶ burst into crying とも言える。

---

buy for a song
動 句 とても安く買う

No one else wanted it, so Mark was able to buy it for a song.

誰もそれを欲しがらなかったので、マークはとても安く買うことができた。

▶▶ for a song で「とても安く」。I could buy this house for a song, because it's so ugly.「見た目がよくなかったから、その家を格安で買えたよ」

---

by a long shot
副 句 インフォーマル かけ離れて、断然

Messi was the best soccer player in the game, by a long shot.

メッシはその試合で、断然最高のサッカー選手だった。

▶▶ 否定文として、She hasn't done her share of the work by a long shot. で、「彼女は自分の仕事を全然やっていなかった」となる。

Let's Review

04 I keep replaying this song. And every time I listen to it, I _____.

僕はこの歌をリプレイし続けている。そしてこの曲を聞くと毎回、急に涙があふれてくるんだ。

05 No one else wanted it, so Mark was able to _____.

誰もそれを欲しがらなかったので、マークはとても安く買うことができた。

06 Messi was the best soccer player in the game, _____.

メッシはその試合で、断然最高のサッカー選手だった。

解答 **04** burst into tears **05** buy it for a song **06** by a long shot

DAY 06

07 by and large
副句 一般的に

By and large, language is a tool for concealing the truth.
一般的に、言葉は真実を隠すための道具だ。

▶▶ 同義として、on the whole、in general がある。

---

08 by chance
副句 偶然

Learning is not attained by chance, it must be sought for with ardor and diligence.
知識は偶然には得られない。情熱と勤勉さをもって追求されなければならない。

▶▶ by ill chance で、「運悪く」という言い方もある。

---

09 by means of
前 ～によって

End Cigarette Smoking by Means of Hypnosis: Have you ever considered attempting to end smoking by hypnotherapy?
『催眠術による禁煙』。催眠術でタバコを止めるという試みを考えたことがありますか。

▶▶ with the use of, owing to と同義。

Let's Review

07 _____, language is a tool for concealing the truth.

一般的に、言葉は真実を隠すための道具だ。

08 Learning is not attained _____, it must be sought for with ardor and diligence.

知識は偶然には得られない。情熱と勤勉さをもって追求されなければならない。

09 End Cigarette Smoking _____ Hypnosis: Have you ever considered attempting to end smoking by hypnotherapy?

『催眠術による禁煙』。催眠術でタバコを止めるという試みを考えたことがありますか。

解答 **07** By and large **08** by chance **09** by Means of

DAY 06

B.Y.O.B
略 **インフォーマル** 酒類は各自ご持参ください

House Party—This Friday 9 P.M., Free Drink, But You're Welcome To B.Y.O.B.

ホームパーティー——今週の金曜日、午後9時、フリードリンク、ただし酒類は各自ご持参ください。

▶▶ 招待状やEメールなど、最後の締めの部分に使われることの多い表現。

---

by oneself
副 **句** 独力で、ひとりで

I want to go watch 'The Avengers: Age of Ultron,' I bet no one will go with me. So I will go by myself.

僕は「アベンジャーズ／エイジ・オブ・ウルトロン」を見にいきたい。誰も一緒にこないこと、うけあいだ。だからひとりで行く。

▶▶ I went there all by myself.「まったくの一人であそこまで行った」のように all を使った強調の表現もよく見られる。

---

by word of mouth
副 **句** 口伝えに

The message reached Mark quietly by word of mouth.

そのメッセージは、口伝えでそっとマークに届けられた。

▶▶ 形容詞として word-of-mouth を名詞の前におけば、word-of-mouth information「口コミ情報」となる。

Let's Review

10 House Party—This Friday 9 P.M., Free Drink, But You're Welcome To _____.

ホームパーティー——今週の金曜日、午後9時、フリードリンク、ただし酒類は各自ご持参ください。

11 I want to go watch 'The Avengers: Age of Ultron,' I bet no one will go with me. So I will go _____.

僕は「アベンジャーズ／エイジ・オブ・ウルトロン」を見にいきたい。誰も一緒にこないこと、うけあいだ。だからひとりで行く。

12 The message reached Mark quietly _____.

そのメッセージは、口伝えでそっとマークに届けられた。

解答 ⑩ B.Y.O.B　⑪ by myself　⑫ by word of mouth

01 call it a day
動句 (その日の仕事を)終わりにする

Let's call it a day and go out for a drink.
今日はこれで終わりにして、飲みにいこう。

▶▶ 昼夜は関係なく、そこで仕事を終わらせようというときに使える。

02 call off
動 中止する

Mark had to call off his birthday party on account of rain.
マークは雨のために自分のバースデイ・パーティーを中止しなければならなかった。

▶▶ イベントをキャンセルするときなどによく使う表現。

03 call on
動 ❶訪ねる

Mark called on Julia while he was in Seoul.
マークはソウルにいる間にジュリアを訪ねた。

❷求める

Eva called on Mark to give some money for the taxi fare to home.
エヴァは、自宅までのタクシー料金としていくらか渡してほしいと、マークに求めた。

▶▶ call on は「ちょっと立ち寄る」、visit は「(社交上必要なので)訪問する」という意味合い。

Let's Review

01 Let's _____ and go out for a drink.

今日はこれで終わりにして、飲みにいこう。

02 Mark had to _____ his birthday party on account of rain.

マークは雨のために自分のバースデイ・パーティーを中止しなければならなかった。

03 Eva _____ Mark to give some money for the taxi fare to home.

エヴァは、自宅までのタクシー料金としていくらか渡してほしいと、マークに求めた。

解答 **01** call it a day **02** call off **03** called on

DAY 07

04 call out
動句 ❶大声で呼ぶ

Eva's name was called out several times, but she was unable to hear it.

エヴァの名前が数回大声で呼ばれたが、彼女はそれが聞こえなかった。

❷呼び出す

Mark's screen just blacked out, so he had to call out an engineer.

マークの画面が真っ暗になったので、彼はエンジニアを呼ばねばならなかった。

▶▶ 2番目の意味は、誰かに助けやサービスを求めるときと覚えるとよい。

---

05 can of worms
名 スラング インフォーマル 込み入った問題

It seems to me that Julia has opened a can of worms here. ジュリアはここで、込み入った問題に触れたように私は思う。

▶▶ Don't open up a can of worms! といえば、「虫入りの缶を開けるな」すなわち「厄介ごとを引き起こすな」となる。

---

06 carry a tune
動句 音を外さずに歌う、正しく歌う

Brian can't carry a tune. ブライアンは音痴だ。

I wish I could sing. I don't wish to be famous. Just to carry a tune would be nice!

歌うことができたらなあ。有名になることは望んでいない。正しい音程で歌うことができるだけで素晴らしいのに！

▶▶ call the tune で「思い通りに方針を決める」の熟語となる。

Let's Review

04 Eva's name was _____ several times, but she was unable to hear it.

エヴァの名前が数回大声で呼ばれたが、彼女はそれが聞こえなかった。

05 It seems to me that Julia has opened a _____ here.

ジュリアはここで、込み入った問題に触れたように私は思う。

06 I wish I could sing. I don't wish to be famous. Just to _____ would be nice!

歌うことができたらなあ。有名になることは望んでいない。正しい音程で歌うことができるだけで素晴らしいのに！

解答　04 called out　05 can of worms　06 carry a tune

carry out
動 実行する、遂行する、成就する

Brian and Mark will carry out their intention to the last.
ブライアンとマークは、自分たちの意志を最後まで遂行するだろう。

▶▶ ただ「実行する」のではなく、完遂し、かつ結論まで持っていくイメージ。

catch it or get it
動 句 インフォーマル 叱られる、罰を受ける、理解する

Mark's son knew he would catch it when he came home late for supper.
マークの息子は、夕飯に遅れて帰宅すると叱られるだろうとわかっていた。

It doesn't matter if your answer is yes or no, you're going to get it anyway.
あなたの答えがイエスでもノーでもどちらでも構わない、どちらにしても理解することになるだろう。

▶▶ 親と子、教師と生徒、上司と部下など、どのような場合でも使える。

catch on
動 インフォーマル （〜の意味を）理解する

I was wondering who would catch on to the lyrics.
誰が歌詞の意味を理解するだろうかと思っていたのですが。

▶▶ I hope our new product catches on with children.「新製品が子どもにウケるといいな」

Let's Review

07 Brian and Mark will _____ their intention to the last.

ブライアンとマークは、自分たちの意志を最後まで遂行するだろう。

08 Mark's son knew he would _____ when he came home late for supper.

マークの息子は、夕飯に遅れて帰宅すると叱られるだろうとわかっていた。

09 I was wondering who would _____ to the lyrics.

誰が歌詞の意味を理解するだろうかと思っていたのですが。

解答 **07** carry out **08** catch it **09** catch on

DAY 07

10 catch one's eye

動 句 目を引く、目を奪う

A great place to be. But unfortunately nothing caught my eye.

素晴らしい場所だ。だが残念なことに、僕の目を引くものは何もなかった。

I believe it was a Tuesday when you caught my eye.

君のことが目に留まったのは、火曜日だったと思う。

▶▶ catch one's attention とほぼ同義。

---

11 catch some rays

動 句 スラング インフォーマル 日を浴びる、日焼けをする

Sun is finally out! Yeah! I have to run out and catch some rays before it disappears again.

太陽がついに出てきた！ やった！ また隠れてしまう前に、外に走っていって日を浴びなくちゃ。

▶▶ ray に「日光」や「太陽の光」の意味がある。

---

12 chain-smoke

動 続けてタバコを吸う

I want to sit by the river and chain-smoke and read some sort of culture book.

僕は川べりに腰かけて、タバコを吸い続け、何か教養のある本を読みたい。

▶▶ 名詞の chain smoker はおなじみ。その動詞形。

Let's Review

10 I believe it was a Tuesday when you _____.

君のことが目に留まったのは、火曜日だったと思う。

11 Sun is finally out! Yeah! I have to run out and _____ before it disappears again.

太陽がついに出てきた！ やった！ また隠れてしまう前に、外に走っていって日を浴びなくちゃ。

12 I want to sit by the river and _____ and read some sort of culture book.

僕は川べりに腰かけて、タバコを吸い続け、何か教養のある本を読みたい。

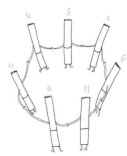

解答 **10** caught my eye   **11** catch some rays   **12** chain-smoke

01 change hands
動句 持ち主が変わる

They are finally putting something new in there. Did you hear that coffee shop changed hands too?

彼らはついに、新しいものをそこに投入しつつある。あのコーヒーショップも所有者が変わったこと、聞いた？

▶▶ 通常、hands と複数形で「管理、所有」の意味となる。

02 change one's tune
動句 インフォーマル 調子を急に変える、急に下手に出る

Eva said she was innocent, but when Mark found the stolen watch in her pocket she changed her tune.

エヴァは自分は無実だと言ったが、マークが彼女のポケットから盗まれた時計を見つけ出すと、急に下手に出た。

▶▶ 「調子をガラッと変える」を sing a different tune ともいう。

03 cheapskate
名 インフォーマル けちんぼ、しみったれ

Julia didn't like to go out on a date with Mark because he is a cheapskate.

マークはけちなので、ジュリアは彼とデートに出かけるのが好きではない。

▶▶ skate には fellow「男、やつ」の意味がある。good skate で「いい人」の意味。

Let's Review

01 They are finally putting something new in there. Did you hear that coffee shop _____ too?

彼らはついに、新しいものをそこに投入しつつある。あのコーヒーショップも所有者が変わったこと、聞いた？

02 Eva said she was innocent, but when Mark found the stolen watch in her pocket she _____.

エヴァは自分は無実だと言ったが、マークが彼女のポケットから盗まれた時計を見つけ出すと、急に下手に出た。

03 Julia didn't like to go out on a date with Mark because he is a _____.

マークはけちなので、ジュリアは彼とデートに出かけるのが好きではない。

解答 **01** changed hands **02** changed her tune **03** cheapskate

DAY 08

chew the fat
動　句　スラング　気楽におしゃべりをする

I think we need a day together next week just to chew the fat.

私たちは来週、気楽におしゃべりだけするために、一緒にいる日が一日必要だと思うわ。

▶▶ 楽しい雰囲気でチャットすること。Let's get together for coffee and chew the fat.「コーヒーでも飲みながら、しゃべろうよ」

chime in
動　インフォーマル　(～と)一致する

Brian was happy, and the dance music chimed in with his feelings.

ブライアンは楽しんでいた、そしてダンス音楽は彼の気持ちと一致していた。

▶▶ 2つの調和が非常に良いことを示す。The illustrations chime in perfectly with the text.「イラストとテキストは本当によくマッチしている」

chip off the old block
名　句　親にそっくりな子

Look at my beautiful girl, chip off the old block, eh?

私の美しい娘を見て、そっくりでしょ、ね？

Mark is becoming a chip off the old block!

マークは父親に似てきている！

▶▶ chip が子どもで、old block が親と理解すればよい。

Let's Review

04 I think we need a day together next week just to _____.

私たちは来週、気楽におしゃべりだけするために、一緒にいる日が一日必要だと思うわ。

05 Brian was happy, and the dance music _____ with his feelings.

ブライアンは楽しんでいた、そしてダンス音楽は彼の気持ちと一致していた。

06 Mark is becoming a _____!

マークは父親に似てきている！

解答 **04** chew the fat **05** chimed in **06** chip off the old block

DAY 08

07 clip one's wings
動 句 活動力を奪う

I won't let fear clip my wings.

僕は、恐怖で動けないなんてことにはならない。

▶▶ 鳥の羽がなくなれば、自由がなくなり、行動できなくなることから。

---

08 closed book
名 さっぱりわからないもの、謎

His early life is a closed book.

彼の若い頃の人生は謎である。

▶▶ open book と言えば、「明白なこと」となる。

---

09 cold shoulder
名 インフォーマル 冷淡な態度

Eva still cares about Mark even though he gives her the cold shoulder sometimes.

マークはエヴァに時々冷たい態度をとるのに、エヴァはまだマークを気にかけている。

▶▶ 「冷たい態度をとる」の意味で、動詞は give の他に show や turn になることもある。

Let's Review

07 I won't let fear _____.

僕は、恐怖で動けないなんてこと
にはならない。

08 His early life is a _____.

彼の若い頃の人生は謎である。

09 Eva still cares about Mark even though he gives her the _____ sometimes.

マークはエヴァに時々冷たい態度をとるのに、エヴァはまだマークを気にかけている。

解答 **07** clip my wings **08** closed book **09** cold shoulder

DAY 08

10 cold snap
名 急な寒さ

Banana prices are expected to soar again in local stores because of heavy rain and a cold snap.
大雨と急な寒さで、地元の店ではまたバナナが急に値上がりする見込みだ。

▶▶ cold spell だと、「異常な寒さが続く」こと。

11 collect dust
動 句 ほこりがたまる

Thousands of wine bottles collect dust while labels await federal approval.
製品が連邦政府の認可を待っている間に、何千本というワインボトルがほこりをかぶっている。

▶▶ 同義で、gather dust も使われる。

12 come about
動 起こる

Sometimes it is hard to tell how an argument comes about.
どのように議論が起こるのかを把握するのが難しい、ということが時々ある。

▶▶ How did this damage come about?「どうしてこんな被害になったのですか？」など、方向性や思っていたのと違う (change) の意味を含む。

Let's Review

10 Banana prices are expected to soar again in local stores because of heavy rain and a _____.

大雨と急な寒さで、地元の店ではまたバナナが急に値上がりする見込みだ。

11 Thousands of wine bottles _____ while labels await federal approval.

製品が連邦政府の認可を待っている間に、何千本というワインボトルがほこりをかぶっている。

12 Sometimes it is hard to tell how an argument _____.

どのように議論が起こるのかを把握するのが難しい、ということが時々ある。

解答 **10** cold snap **11** collect dust **12** comes about

01 come again
動 インフォーマル もう一回言ってください

"What? Come again," Julia said.

「何でしょうか？ もう一回言ってください」とジュリアは言った。

▶▶ What did you say?「何と言ったのですか？」と聞こえなくて使う場合と、I can't believe you said that.「何だと？ もう一度言ってみろ」と腹を立てている場合がある。

02 come alive
動 インフォーマル 生き生きと活動する

Mark comes alive in the night time.

マークは夜に生き生きと活動する。

▶▶ come to life と同義。

03 come by
動 手に入れる

Genuine people are hard to come by while good friends are even harder to find.

誠実な人と知り合うのは難しく、良い友人を見つけるのはさらに難しい。

How did Eva come by that money?

エヴァはどうやってあの金を手に入れたんだ？

▶▶ come by something（お金、富、品物など）or someone の形で使われる。A good assistant is hard to come by.「優れたアシスタントを見つけるのは難しい」

Let's Review

01 "What? _____,"
Julia said.

「何でしょうか? もう一回言ってください」とジュリアは言った。

02 Mark _____ in the night time.

マークは夜に生き生きと活動する。

03 Genuine people are hard to _____ while good friends are even harder to find.

誠実な人と知り合うのは難しく、良い友人を見つけるのはさらに難しい。

解答 **01** Come again   **02** comes alive   **03** come by

DAY 09

come out in the open
名 句 明らかになる

The truth will always come out in the open. It's just a matter of time.　真実は常に明らかになる。時間の問題にすぎない。

▶▶ come out into the open も同じ。

---

come out with
動 句　❶発表する

Mark came out with a clear declaration of his principles.
マークは自分の主義を明確に宣言した。

❷外に出てくる

When he is mad, the truth comes out with a lot of bullshit.　彼が怒ると、たくさんのでたらめと共に真実が現れる。

▶▶ Come out with it!「しゃべってしまえ」「さっさと言ってしまえ」の意味で使える。

---

come through for
動 句　〜を支える、〜の要求に応える

My friends always come through for me.
友人たちはいつでも、私を支えてくれる。

If you don't come through for me then don't expect me to do the same for you.
あなたが私の要求に応じてくれないなら、私もあなたの要求に応じると思わないで。

▶▶ for の後は人がくる。特に難しい状況に立たされた人を助けるというニュアンスがある。

Let's Review

 The truth will always _____.
It's just a matter of time.

真実は常に明らかになる。時間の問題にすぎない。

 When he is mad, the truth _____ a lot of bullshit.

彼が怒ると、たくさんのでたらめと共に真実が現れる。

 My friends always _____ me.

友人たちはいつでも、私を支えてくれる。

解答　04 come out in the open　05 come out with　06 come through for

07 come to light
動 句 明るみに出る、知れ渡る

Don't worry about what someone does behind your back because it will come to light.

自分の背後で誰が何をしているかなど心配するな、なぜならそれは明るみに出てくるから。

▶▶ Nothing new has come to light since we talked last.「最後に話してから、何にも新しいことは出てきてないよ」

08 come up with
動 句 思いつく

At this point in my life, I should probably have some goals or something. I might try to come up with one.

人生の現時点で、私はおそらく何らかの目標のようなものを持つべきなのだろう。それを見つけるようにしてみようかな。

▶▶ think of と同義。

09 common ground
名 共通点、見解の一致する点

Come talk with me. Let's find some common ground.

来て一緒に話そう。見解の一致する点を見つけよう。

▶▶ mutual understanding と同義。

Let's Review

07 Don't worry about what someone does behind your back because it will _____.

自分の背後で誰が何をしているかなど心配するな、なぜならそれは明るみに出てくるから。

08 At this point in my life, I should probably have some goals or something. I might try to _____ one.

人生の現時点で、私はおそらく何らかの目標のようなものを持つべきなのだろう。それを見つけるようにしてみようかな。

09 Come talk with me. Let's find some _____.

来て一緒に話そう。見解の一致する点を見つけよう。

解答　**07** come to light　**08** come up with　**09** common ground

DAY 09

 common touch

名 親しみやすさ

I think the most important thing a leader should have is the common touch.

リーダーが持つべきもっとも大事なものは、親しみやすさだと思う。

▶▶ (権力者・高貴な人・有名人)の親しみやすさ、庶民性を「ほめる」意味で使う。

---

 compare notes

動 インフォーマル 意見を交換し合う

Mark had a fun lunch yesterday at Apple Bee's with Julia where they compared notes.

マークは昨日、ジュリアとアップルビーで楽しくランチをとり、意見を交換し合った。

▶▶ 片方から一方的に話す場合は compare notes とは言えない。双方ともに知っていること、やったことがあることに関してお互いに話すことが前提。

---

 cool as a cucumber

形 句 インフォーマル 非常に冷静で

Julia is the queen of a confrontation and remaining cool as a cucumber.

ジュリアは対決の女王であり、非常に冷静なままである。

▶▶ as cool as a cucumber でも使える。

Let's Review

10 I think the most important thing a leader should have is the

_____.

リーダーが持つべきもっとも大事なものは、親しみやすさだと思う。

11 Mark had a fun lunch yesterday at Apple Bee's with Julia where they _____.

マークは昨日、ジュリアとアップルビーで楽しくランチをとり、意見を交換し合った。

12 Julia is the queen of a confrontation and remaining

_____.

ジュリアは対決の女王であり、非常に冷静なままである。

解答 **10** common touch　**11** compared notes　**12** cool as a cucumber

DAY 10

01 cool customer
名 冷静沈着な人

Julia never gets too excited about anything. She is a cool customer.

ジュリアはどんなことにも決して興奮しすぎることはない。冷静沈着な人間だ。

▶▶ customer は「顧客」の意味ではなく、「人」のこと。

02 coop up
動句 閉じ込められる

I was cooped up in the house and did tons of homework all day.

僕は家に閉じ込められて、一日中、大量の宿題をやった。

▶▶ coop は名詞で「(小動物の)小屋」、そこからとても「狭いところ」の意に転じた。

03 cop out
動句 スラング インフォーマル 手を引く、逃れる

Mark copped out of my coworker's retirement party.

マークは僕の同僚の退職パーティーから逃げた。

▶▶ The students copped out of cleaning up after the party.「学生はパーティーの後の掃除をしないで帰った」のように、すべきことや約束事から逃れること。

Let's Review

01 Julia never gets too excited about anything. She is a _____.

ジュリアはどんなことにも決して興奮しすぎることはない。冷静沈着な人間だ。

02 I was _____ in the house and did tons of homework all day.

僕は家に閉じ込められて、一日中、大量の宿題をやった。

03 Mark _____ of my coworker's retirement party.

マークは僕の同僚の退職パーティーから逃げた。

解答 **01** cool customer **02** cooped up **03** copped out

DAY 10

04 copy cat
名 真似をする人

Brian was trying to be a copy cat of Daniel Craig.
ブライアンは、ダニエル・クレイグの真似をしようとしていた。

▶▶ Don't be a copycat. で「人(猿)まねはやめろ！」

---

05 couch potato
名 カウチポテト、テレビばかり見ている怠け者

I used to watch TV all day long when I was a couch potato.
私はカウチポテト族だったとき、一日中テレビを見ていたものです。

▶▶ sofa (=couch) spud (=potate) の言い方もある。

---

06 couldn't care less
動 句 インフォーマル まったく気にしない、少しも関係ない

I couldn't care less about what anyone is doing.
私は、誰が何をしていようがまったく気にしない。

There are six billion people in the world, but I couldn't care less. There is only one that I need.
世界中には60億人の人がいるが、私には少しも関係ない。必要な存在はたったひとりなの。

▶▶ まったくに気にしないことから、「痛くも痒くもない」こと。

Let's Review

04 Brian was trying to be a _____ of Daniel Craig.

ブライアンは、ダニエル・クレイグの真似をしようとしていた。

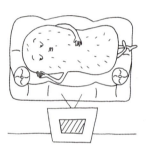

05 I used to watch TV all day long when I was a _____.

私はカウチポテト族だったとき、一日中テレビを見ていたものです。

06 I _____ about what anyone is doing.

私は、誰が何をしていようがまったく気にしない。

解答 **04** copy cat **05** couch potato **06** couldn't care less

DAY 10

07 count on
動 〜をあてにする

I came to the conclusion that I can only count on my wife in my life.

僕が人生で頼れるのは、ただひとり妻だけだという結論にいたった。

▶▶ You can count on me. で「任せておいて／大丈夫だよ」、I was counting on you. といえば、「期待してたのになぁ〜」となる。

---

08 cover up
動 インフォーマル 〜をかばう、隠す

I believe dinosaurs were lies, to cover up the existence of Pokemon.

僕は、恐竜はごまかしで、ポケモンの存在を隠すためだったと信じている。

▶▶ Cover yourself up.「(はだかの人に)何か着なさい」

---

09 cozy up
動 スラング 〜と近づきになる、親しくなろうとする

Eva is cozying up to Mark so she can join the club.

エヴァはそのクラブに入れるよう、マークと親しくなろうとしている。

▶▶ 「cozy up + to + 人」の形をとる。

Let's Review

07 I came to the conclusion that I can only _____ my wife in my life.

僕が人生で頼れるのは、ただひとり妻だけだという結論にいたった。

08 I believe dinosaurs were lies, to _____ the existence of Pokemon.

僕は、恐竜はごまかしで、ポケモンの存在を隠すためだったと信じている。

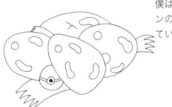

09 Eva is _____ to Mark so she can join the club.

エヴァはそのクラブに入れるよう、マークと親しくなろうとしている。

解答 **07** count on   **08** cover up   **09** cozying up

DAY 10

10 crack a book
動　句　スラング　勉強する

I should crack a book for Physics, also I should face the interview.
僕は物理の勉強をすべきだし、面接にも立ち向かうべきだ。

▶▶ She didn't crack a book all semester.「彼女は学期中、本を開いて勉強することはなかった」など、否定文で使うことが多い。

11 crack a joke
動　句　インフォーマル　冗談を言う

If I crack a joke, he'll never get it.
僕が冗談を言っても、彼には決してわからないだろう。

▶▶ (tell, make) a joke about 〜 で「〜についてジョークを言う、軽口をたたく」。

12 crack the whip
動　句　インフォーマル　きびしく支配(命令)する

I love my team but we need a strong male boot camp type manager to crack the whip.
私はチームが大好きだが、チームをきびしく指導する、ブートキャンプにいるような強い男性マネージャーが必要だ。

▶▶ 権力・権威を持つ人が、命令して従わせる状況を指す。

Let's Review

10 I should _____ for Physics, also I should face the interview.

僕は物理の勉強をすべきだし、面接にも立ち向かうべきだ。

11 If I _____, he'll never get it.

僕が冗談を言っても、彼には決してわからないだろう。

12 I love my team but we need a strong male boot camp type manager to _____.

私はチームが大好きだが、チームをきびしく指導する、ブートキャンプにいるような強い男性マネージャーが必要だ。

解答 **10** crack a book **11** crack a joke **12** crack the whip

01 **not all cracked up to be**
副 句　評判ほどではない、大したものではない

Traveling with a baby is not all cracked up to be. But not the way you think.

赤ん坊と一緒に旅行をするのは、大したことではない。だが、君が考えているようなものではないよ。

▶▶ be cracked up to be で、「〜という評判である、〜と信じられている」の意味。

---

02 **creep up on**
動　忍び寄る

Time doesn't make sense to me. Finals have crept up on me.

僕には、時間は理にかなったものではない。期末試験が忍び寄ってきている。

▶▶ The cat crept up on the mouse.「猫がネズミにそぉーっと近づいた」

---

03 **crocodile tears**
名　そら涙、うそ泣き

I would never tell you lies and no crocodile tears.

僕は君に決してうそをつかないだろうし、うそ泣きもしない。

▶▶ ワニがうそ泣きをするという言い伝えがあることからできた表現。

Let's Review

01 Traveling with a baby is _____. But not the way you think.

赤ん坊と一緒に旅行をするのは、大したことではない。だが、君が考えているようなものではないよ。

02 Time doesn't make sense to me. Finals have _____ me.

僕には、時間は理にかなったものではない。期末試験が忍び寄ってきている。

03 I would never tell you lies and no _____.

僕は君に決してうそをつかないだろうし、うそ泣きもしない。

解答 **01** not all cracked up to be **02** crept up on **03** crocodile tears

04 **crop up**
動 思いがけず生じる

A problem cropped up while Mark was away.

マークが不在のとき、思いがけずある問題が生じた。

▶▶ いい意味で「突然出てくる」の意味もある。"I left my glassess." "They will crop up."「メガネを置き忘れちゃった」「すぐに出てくるよ!」

---

05 **cross one's path**
動 句 偶然出会う

Surprisingly, Julia crossed Mark's path in Central Park one afternoon.

驚いたことに、ジュリアはある午後、セントラル・パークでマークとばったり出会った。

▶▶ If he ever crosses my path, I will kill him.「もし彼が私の前にもう一度現れたら、殺すわ!」と、偶然とはいえ出会いたくない場合も使える。

---

06 **cross swords**
動 句 文 論争する

Mark didn't want to cross swords with Eva any more.

マークは、これ以上エヴァと論争したくなかった。

▶▶ 「剣を交える」ことから、実際には「議論を戦わせる」の意味となる。

Let's Review

04 A problem _____ while Mark was away.

マークが不在のとき、思いがけずある問題が生じた。

05 Surprisingly, Julia _____ in Central Park one afternoon.

驚いたことに、ジュリアはある午後、セントラル・パークでマークとばったり出会った。

06 Mark didn't want to _____ with Eva any more.

マークは、これ以上エヴァと論争したくなかった。

解答 **04** cropped up　**05** crossed Mark's path　**06** cross swords

07 cry on one's shoulder
動 句 愚痴を言う、打ち明ける

You can cry on my shoulder. I am here for you.
僕に愚痴を言っていいんだ。君のためにここにいるよ。

Eva needed a shoulder to cry on.
エヴァは、頼ることができる人を必要としていた。

▶▶ shoulder to cry on で、「悩みを聞いてくれる人」の意味となる。

08 cut a class
動 句 授業を休む

Brian cut a class with permission from the professor.
ブライアンは、教授の許可を得て講義を休んだ。

▶▶ 特定の授業であれば、to cut the English class「英語の授業を欠席する」となる。

09 cut a deal
動 句 協定を結ぶ、取引をする

Did you cut a deal?　君たちは協定を結んだの？
Could you cut me a deal?　取引をしませんか？

▶▶ cut が「切る」の意味から、cut a deal も「取り引きを切る（結ばない）」にはならないことに注意。cut には「分け合う」といった意味がある。

Let's Review

07 You can _____.
I am here for you.

僕に愚痴を言っていいんだ。君のためにここにいるよ。

08 Brian _____ with permission from the professor.

ブライアンは、教授の許可を得て講義を休んだ。

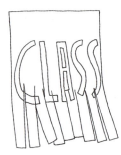

09 Did you _____?

君たちは協定を結んだの？

解答　**07** cry on my shoulder　**08** cut a class　**09** cut a deal

❿ cut corners
動句 ❶近道する

Mark cut corners going home in hurry.

マークは近道をして、急いで家に帰った。

❷手を抜く

I don't cut corners. I don't beat around the bush.

僕は手を抜かない。遠まわしな言い方をしない。

▶▶ Don't cut corners. といえば、「しっかりとやってくれ」となる。

⓫ cut one's throat
動句 インフォーマル 自滅する

Eva cut her own throat by her carelessness.

エヴァは自分の不注意で自滅した。

▶▶「自分の首を絞める」の意味で使える。

⓬ cut the mustard
動句 スラング 成功する、いい成績を収める

Our president resigns, he just couldn't cut the mustard.

当社の社長が辞任する。いい業績を収められなかったのだ。

▶▶ mustard(カラシ)の種はなかなか切れないこと(切れた＝期待に沿う)が由来とも言われる。

Let's Review

10 Mark _____ going home in hurry.

マークは近道をして、急いで家に帰った。

11 Eva _____ by her carelessness.

エヴァは自分の不注意で自滅した。

12 Our president resigns, he just couldn't _____.

当社の社長が辞任する。いい業績を収められなかったのだ。

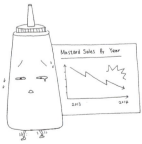

解答 **10** cut corners　**11** cut her own throat　**12** cut the mustard

DAY 12

01 cut up
動 ❶（通例受け身で）悲しませる

Mark was badly cut up when Julia gave him back his ring. ジュリアが指輪をマークに返したとき、彼はひどく悲しんだ。

❷ふざけ回る、滑稽に行動する

Brian would always cut up if there were any girls watching.
ブライアンは、女性が近くにいるときはいつもふざけた行動をする。

▶▶「細く切る」「破壊する」「こき下ろす」など、他にも様々な意味がある cup up。文脈から最適な意味を見つけよう。

02 dare say
動 句 あえて言う

It's a good story, but I dare say it's apocryphal.
それはいい話だけど、あえて言うなら疑わしい。

▶▶ 反語的なニュアンスをこめて、You are tired, I dare say. で、「きっと疲れているのだろう」の意味になる。

03 dark horse
名 インフォーマル ダークホース、意外な存在

House of Cards is a dark horse candidate for favorite drama of the year.
ハウス・オブ・カードは、「今年もっとも好きなドラマ」の意外な候補だ。

▶▶ dark horse candidate で、「意外な候補」となる。

Let's Review

01 Mark was badly _____ when Julia gave him back his ring.

ジュリアが指輪をマークに返したとき、彼はひどく悲しんだ。

02 It's a good story, but I _____ it's apocryphal.

それはいい話だけど、あえて言うなら疑わしい。

03 House of Cards is a _____ candidate for favorite drama of the year.

ハウス・オブ・カードは、「今年もっとも好きなドラマ」の意外な候補だ。

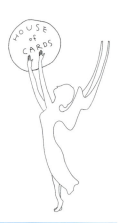

解答 **01** cut up **02** dare say **03** dark horse

DAY 12

04 dash light
名 計器灯

Car's dash light came on and the fuel gauge isn't working. This seems bad.
車の計器灯がつき、燃料計は作動していない。これはやっかいな感じだ。

▶▶ dash は dashboard「ダッシュボード（計器盤）」のこと。

05 day by day
副 一日ごとに

You can't change everything overnight, but you can always change it slowly, day by day, one by one.
一晩ですべてを変えることはできないけれど、ゆっくりと常に変えることはできる、一日ごとに、ひとつずつ。

▶▶ 形容詞的に使うときは、day-by-day ＋名詞。

06 day in and day out
副 句 来る日も来る日も

Success is the sum of small efforts, repeated day in and day out.
成功とは、来る日も来る日も繰り返される、小さな努力の総量だ。

▶▶ 形容詞的に使うときは、day-in and day-out ＋名詞。

Let's Review

04 Car's _____ came on and the fuel gauge isn't working. This seems bad.

車の計器灯がつき、燃料計は作動していない。これはやっかいな感じだ。

05 You can't change everything overnight, but you can always change it slowly, _____, one by one.

一晩ですべてを変えることはできないけれど、ゆっくりと常に変えることはできる、一日ごとに、ひとつずつ。

06 Success is the sum of small efforts, repeated _____.

成功とは、来る日も来る日も繰り返される、小さな努力の総量だ。

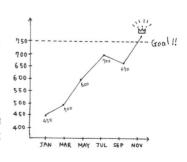

解答　**04** dash light　**05** day by day　**06** day in and day out

DAY 12

day of reckoning
名 句 決算日、報いを受ける時

Oh dear. The day of reckoning has arrived.
なんということ。報いを受ける日が来てしまった。

▶▶ 語源は聖書の「最後の審判の日(The Last Judgement)」から。

---

days are numbered
先が見えている、在任も長くない

Her days as a manager of the company are numbered.
その会社のマネージャーとしての彼女の在任は長くない。

▶▶ 終わりまでの日数が限られていることから病人であれば「余命がいくばくもない」ことになる。

---

dead duck
名 スラング 見込みのない、だめな(人)

When the baseball player broke his arm, he was a dead duck.
その野球選手は腕を折ったとき、見込みがなくなった。

▶▶ duck を使った表現には、sitting duck で「だましやすい人」、lame duck で「死に体」など。

Let's Review

07 Oh dear. The _____ has arrived.

なんということ。報いを受ける日が来てしまった。

08 Her _____ as a manager of the company _____.

その会社のマネージャーとしての彼女の在任は長くない。

09 When the baseball player broke his arm, he was a _____.

その野球選手は腕を折ったとき、見込みがなくなった。

解答 **07** day of reckoning　**08** days, are numbered　**09** dead duck

DAY 12

10 dead to the world
形 句 インフォーマル ❶熟睡して

I'm leaving now to be dead to the world for a couple of hours.　もう行くよ、数時間ぐっすり眠るためにね。

❷意識を失って

McGwire was hit on the head by a baseball and was dead to the world for two hours.

マクガイアは野球のボールが頭に当たって、２時間意識を失っていた。

「昨晩は爆睡したよ」と言いたければ、I was dead to the world last night. となる。

11 dear me
間 おやまあ

Dear me, can you not cry just for a sec?

おやまあ、ちょっとの間泣くのを止められないのかい？

驚き、驚嘆、失望、感心、同情、あきれるなど、文脈によって表す意味も違ってくることに注意。

12 diamond in the rough
名 句 原石のダイヤ

There's so much junk and trash out there. But there's always a diamond in the rough.

そこには非常に多くのくずやごみがある。だが、原石のダイヤも常にある。

ダイヤモンドの原石は、研磨していく工程がなければその本来の美しさを発見できないことからきている。

Let's Review

10 McGwire was hit on the head by a baseball and was _____ for two hours.

マクガイアは野球のボールが頭に当たって、2時間意識を失っていた。

11 _____, can you not cry just for a sec?

おやまあ、ちょっとの間泣くのを止められないのかい？

12 There's so much junk and trash out there. But there's always a _____.

そこには非常に多くのくずやごみがある。だが、原石のダイヤも常にある。

解答　**10** dead to the world　**11** Dear me　**12** diamond in the rough

DAY 13

01 die on the vine
動 句 実を結ばずに終わる

They're going to let this die on the vine if we don't press it.
僕たちがそれに圧力をかけないと、実を結ばずに終わるのを許すことになるぞ。

▶▶ vine は「ぶどうの蔦、ツル」で、「豊饒［大地に作物が実ること］」のイメージを表す。

02 dirt cheap
形 格安の

Fired travel agent reveals how to get dirt cheap airfare tickets.
クビになった旅行代理店の元社員が、格安の飛行機チケットを手に入れる方法を明かしている。

▶▶ どこにでもある土ほどに安いの意味から。

03 dish the dirt
動 句 スラング (人の)悪いうわさ話をする

You secretly dish the dirt on all of us to her, don't you?
君は彼女に対して、僕たち全員のことを密かに悪く言っているよね、そうだろう？

▶▶ dish は「おしゃべりをする」「噂話をする」の意味があり、dirt は「土」のほかに、「ゴシップ・スキャンダル・噂」などの意味がある。

Let's Review

01 They're going to let this _____ if we don't press it.

僕たちがそれに圧力をかけないと、実を結ばずに終わるのを許すことになるぞ。

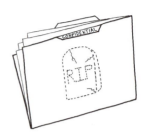

02 Fired travel agent reveals how to get _____ airfare tickets.

クビになった旅行代理店の元社員が、格安の飛行機チケットを手に入れる方法を明かしている。

03 You secretly _____ on all of us to her, don't you?

君は彼女に対して、僕たち全員のことを密かに悪く言っているよね、そうだろう？

解答　**01** die on the vine　**02** dirt cheap　**03** dish the dirt

04 do a double take
動 句 インフォーマル (はっと驚いて) 見直す

Eva's shorts were so short, I had to do a double take to make sure they weren't her panties.

エヴァのショートパンツはとても短くて、それが下着じゃないことを確かめるために見直さなきゃならなかった。

▶▶ 驚くべき光景または信じられないようなときに使う。

05 do away with
動 〜を取り除く

The best way to do away with unwanted facial hair; many women of all ages suffer from unwanted facial hair.

顔の不要なうぶ毛を取り除く最良の方法。あらゆる年齢層の多くの女性たちが、顔の不要なうぶ毛に悩まされています。

▶▶ Let's do away with formalities. で「堅苦しいことはなしにしましょう」という使い方もできる。

06 doggy bag
名 句 持ち帰り袋 (容器)

May I have a doggy bag, please?

持ち帰るための容器をいただけますか？

▶▶ お持ち帰りを頼むときは、ask for a doggy bag で良い。

Let's Review

04 Eva's shorts were so short, I had to _____ to make sure they weren't her panties.

エヴァのショートパンツはとても短くて、それが下着じゃないことを確かめるために見直さなきゃならなかった。

05 The best way to _____ unwanted facial hair; many women of all ages suffer from unwanted facial hair.

顔の不要なうぶ毛を取り除く最良の方法。あらゆる年齢層の多くの女性たちが、顔の不要なうぶ毛に悩まされています。

06 May I have a _____, please?

持ち帰るための容器をいただけますか？

解答 **04** do a double take　**05** do away with　**06** doggy bag

DAY 13

07 doll up
動 スラング 着飾る、めかし込む

I don't understand how some people doll up every morning.

毎朝めかし込んでいる人たちもいるが、なぜそうするのか理解できない。

▶▶ 同義で、pretty up とも言える。

---

08 do or die
形 死に物狂いで

I really cannot afford to get sick right now. I have a huge presentation tomorrow, do or die.

いま、病気になっている余裕はほんとうにない。明日は途方もないプレゼンテーションがあるんだ、死に物狂いでやる。

▶▶ 成功するために死ぬ気でやること。

---

09 double up
動 ❶（身体を）折り曲げさせる

The baseball player was hit by the baseball and doubled up with pain.

その野球選手は野球ボールが当たって、苦痛で身体を折り曲げた。

❷（部屋などを）一緒に使う、分け合う

When Mark came for a visit, Julia had to double up with her sister.

マークが来たとき、ジュリアは妹と部屋を一緒に使わねばならなかった。

▶▶ double up in pain で、「痛みで屈み込む」となる。

Let's Review

07 I don't understand how some people _____ every morning.

毎朝めかし込んでいる人たちもいるが、なぜそうするのか理解できない。

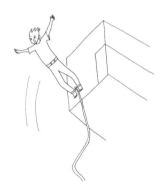

08 I really cannot afford to get sick right now. I have a huge presentation tomorrow, _____.

いま、病気になっている余裕はほんとうにない。明日は途方もないプレゼンテーションがあるんだ、死に物狂いでやる。

09 The baseball player was hit by the baseball and _____ with pain.

その野球選手は野球ボールが当たって、苦痛で身体を折り曲げた。

解答　**07** doll up　**08** do or die　**09** doubled up

DAY 13

down and out
形 句 落ちぶれて、一文なしで

Would you love me if I was down and out?
僕が一文なしだったとしても、僕を愛するかい？

▶▶ down at heel「みすぼらしい」や、down in the mouth「しょげて、がっくりして」の表現もある。

---

draw a blank
動 句 インフォーマル 思い出せない、失敗に終わる

I've been learning Spanish to communicate with his family and then bam! When I met his dad I drew a blank.
彼の家族と話すためにスペイン語をずっと習ってきて、そしてバン！ 彼のお父さんと会ったときに、思い出せなかった。

▶▶ blank「白紙、からくじ」を draw「引く」ことから、失敗したり、急に何も思い出せなくなる状態を表す。

---

drift off
動 句 いつの間にか

That annoying moment when you finally drift off to sleep and your phone obnoxiously vibrates.
いつの間にかようやく眠りに落ちた時に、はた迷惑にも電話が振動するのは、気に障る瞬間だ。

▶▶ drift off to sleep という塊の表現として覚えると便利。

Let's Review

10 Would you love me if I was _____?

僕が一文なしだったとしても、僕を愛するかい？

11 I've been learning Spanish to communicate with his family and then bam! When I met his dad I _____.

彼の家族と話すためにスペイン語をずっと習ってきて、そしてバン！ 彼のお父さんと会ったときに、思い出せなかった。

12 That annoying moment when you finally _____ to sleep and your phone obnoxiously vibrates.

いつの間にかようやく眠りに落ちた時に、はた迷惑にも電話が振動するのは、気に障る瞬間だ。

解答　**10** down and out　**11** draw a blank　**12** drift off

01 drink down
動句 飲み下す、飲み干す

Mark was so thirsty that he drank down six glasses of juice.
マークはとてものどが渇いていたので、ジュースをグラス6杯飲みほした。

▶▶ 飲み物だけでなく、Drink down this medicine. といえば、「薬は完全に呑みこめ」という意味になる。

02 drink like a fish
動句 大酒飲みである

Julia admires people who genuinely love healthy food but Mark likes to eat junk food and drink like a fish.
ジュリアは、ヘルシーな食事が心から大好きな人たちを称賛しているが、マークはジャンクフードが好きで、大酒飲みである。

▶▶ eat like a horse「大食いをする」と合わせて覚えておこう。

03 drive one crazy
動句 インフォーマル イライラさせる、怒らせる

My aunt drives me crazy. I am pretty sure she doesn't want me to sleep.
伯母は私をイライラさせる。彼女は私を眠らせたくないのに違いない。

▶▶ 他にも drive (someone) mad, angry, nervous などが使える。

Let's Review

01 Mark was so thirsty that he _____ six glasses of juice.

マークはとてものどが渇いていたので、ジュースをグラス6杯飲みほした。

02 Julia admires people who genuinely love healthy food but Mark likes to eat junk food and _____.

ジュリアは、ヘルシーな食事が心から大好きな人たちを称賛しているが、マークはジャンクフードが好きで、大酒飲みである。

03 My aunt _____. I am pretty sure she doesn't want me to sleep.

伯母は私をイライラさせる。彼女は私を眠らせたくないのに違いない。

解答 **01** drank down **02** drink like a fish **03** drives me crazy

DAY 14

04 dropout
名 中退者

Alice is having a hard time getting a better job as she was a high-school dropout.

アリスは高校を中退しているので、よい仕事を得るのに苦労している。

▶▶ 生徒・学生の中退率が高い学校や教育制度を dropout factory「落ちこぼれ生産工場」と言う。

05 drown out
動 押し流す、かき消す

Julia's reply was drowned out by a passing sports car.

ジュリアの答えは、通り過ぎるスポーツカーでかき消された。

▶▶ Don't let the noise of others' opinions drown out your own inner voice.「他人の雑音で自らの内なる声をかき消さないように」とはスティーブ・ジョブズの名言。

06 duck out
動 句 帰る

I am sorry for that I had to duck out before drinks but it was great to connect with you all today.

飲む前に帰らなくちゃならなかったのは残念だけれど、今日は一日中、君と気持ちがつながっていたのは素晴らしかった。

▶▶ duck には、「素早く動く」の意味がある。

Let's Review

04 Alice is having a hard time getting a better job as she was a high-school _____.

アリスは高校を中退しているので、よい仕事を得るのに苦労している。

05 Julia's reply was _____ by a passing sports car.

ジュリアの答えは、通り過ぎるスポーツカーでかき消された。

06 I am sorry for that I had to _____ before drinks but it was great to connect with you all today.

飲む前に帰らなくちゃならなかったのは残念だけれど、今日は一日中、君と気持ちがつながっていたのは素晴らしかった。

解答　**04** dropout　**05** drowned out　**06** duck out

07 dying to
形 句 どうしても〜したい、〜したくてたまらない

I'm dying to tell you I love you.
君を愛していると、どうしても伝えたい。

I'm dying to know what people think about me.
人々が僕のことをどう考えているのか、知りたくてたまらない。

▶▶ I'm dying to +動詞で、「死ぬほど〜したい」となり、want to +動詞よりずっと強い欲求を表す。

08 ear to the ground
名 句 インフォーマル （地面に耳をつけて地響きを聞くことから）世の中の動きにアンテナを張る

If you have had your ear to the ground, you'll know the truth.
君が世の中の動きにアンテナを張っていたのなら、真実がわかるだろう。

▶▶ I have one's ear to the ground の形で使う。

09 easygoing
形 おおらかな

Because Mark has an easygoing personality, everybody loves him.
マークはおおらかな性格なので、みんな彼が大好きだ。

▶▶ 日本語の「イージーゴーイング」には「安易な、いい加減な」といったマイナスの意味合いもあるが、英語の easygoing にネガティブなニュアンスはない。

Let's Review

07 I'm _____ tell you I love you.
君を愛していると、どうしても伝えたい。

08 If you have had your _____, you'll know the truth.

君が世の中の動きにアンテナを張っていたのなら、真実がわかるだろう。

09 Because Mark has an _____ personality, everybody loves him.

マークはおおらかな性格なので、みんな彼が大好きだ。

解答 **07** dying to　**08** ear to the ground　**09** easygoing

DAY 14

10 easy come, easy go
インフォーマル 得やすいものは失いやすい、悪銭身につかず

Easy come, easy go. That's just how you live.
悪銭身につかず。まさに君の生き方だ。

▶▶ 「あぶく銭は身につかない」という諺があるように、簡単に入ってくるものは、同じく簡単に出て行くの意味。

11 eat like a bird
動 句 とても小食である

I lost weight because lately I've been eating like a bird.
この頃とても小食なので、体重が減った。

▶▶ 小鳥が小さなくちばしでついばむ様子を思い浮かべよう。

12 eat like a horse
動 句 大食いする

Whenever exams come along, I eat like a horse.
テストがやってくると、いつでも僕は大量に食べる。

▶▶ drink like a fish は「大酒飲み」。

Let's Review

10 _____.
That's just how you live.

悪銭身につかず。まさに君の生き方だ。

11 I lost weight because lately I've been _____.

この頃とても小食なので、体重が減った。

12 Whenever exams come along, I _____.

テストがやってくると、いつでも僕は大量に食べる。

解答 **10** easy come, easy go   **11** eating like a bird   **12** eat like a horse

01 every cloud has a silver lining

ことわざ どんなに困難な時にもよいことは必ずある

It is true what they say 'Every cloud has a silver lining.'

「どんなに困難な時にもよいことは必ずある」というのはほんとうだ。

▶▶ silver lining は「銀色に輝く裏地＝希望の光」の意で、「逆境にあっても光がさす」「悪い事があっても何かしらの良いことがある」という諺。

02 eyes pop out

インフォーマル 目が飛び出すほど驚く

When Julia found new CHANEL bags under the Christmas tree, her eyes popped out.

クリスマスツリーの下に新しいシャネルのバッグを見つけたとき、ジュリアは目が飛び出すほど驚いた。

▶▶ one's eyes pop out with astonishment の表現でよく使われる。

03 fair-weather friend

名 句 頼りがいのない友、いい時だけの友だち

There is nothing worse than a fair-weather friend. Figuring out I have a few of those around.

頼りがいのない友ほど最悪なものはない。周りにいるうち数人がそうだとわかった。

▶▶ 反意語は rainy-day friend で「雨の日でも助けてくれる頼りがいのある友」のこと。

Let's Review

01 It is true what they say
'_____.'

「どんなに困難な時にもよいことは必ずある」というのはほんとうだ。

02 When Julia found new CHANEL bags under the Christmas tree, her _____.

クリスマスツリーの下に新しいシャネルのバッグを見つけたとき、ジュリアは目が飛び出すほど驚いた。

03 There is nothing worse than a _____. Figuring out I have a few of those around.

頼りがいのない友ほど最悪なものはない。周りにいるうち数人がそうだとわかった。

解答 **01** Every cloud has a silver lining **02** eyes popped out **03** fair-weather friend

DAY 15

04 fall flat
動 インフォーマル 失敗する

Brian's joke fell flat because no one understood it.
ブライアンのジョークは、誰も理解できなかったために受けなかった。

▶▶ 真っ平らに倒れることから、「まったく反応がない」「完全に失敗する」の意となる。

---

05 fall guy
名 スラング だまされやすい人、かも

He's a fall guy. I'm the brains of the organization.
彼はだまされやすい。僕が組織のブレーンだ。

▶▶ dupe, scapegoat と同義。

---

06 far cry
名 大違い

Mark is a far cry from Julia.
マークはジュリアとは大違いだ。

▶▶ 単に距離が遠い場合は、It's a far cry to Tokyo.「東京まではとても遠い」のように使う。

Let's Review

04 Brian's joke _____ because no one understood it.

ブライアンのジョークは、誰も理解できなかったために受けなかった。

05 He's a _____. I'm the brains of the organization.

彼はだまされやすい。僕が組織のブレーンだ。

06 Mark is a _____ from Julia.

マークはジュリアとは大違いだ。

解答 **04** fell flat   **05** fall guy   **06** far cry

DAY 15

07 fed up
インフォーマル スラング うんざりしている、いやになっている

Sometimes I get fed up with everything. I just want to run away somewhere, someplace where I won't get hurt anymore.

時々、すべてがいやになることがある。どこかに走っていきたい、もう傷つけられることのないどこかに。

 fed が feed「食べる」の過去分詞であることから、「お腹いっぱい」が「飽き飽きしている」「うんざりしている」の意味に転じた。

08 feel down
動 句 落ち込む、元気がない

Focus on yourself, your life and your goals first. Love and the rest will follow; I try to remind myself of this when I feel down about it.

「自分自身、自分の人生、自分の目標にまず集中すること。愛やほかのことは、それについてくるだろう。」落ち込むと、このことを思い出すようにしている。

 feel down の後は前置詞 about がくることが多い。I'm feeling down. で「落ち込んでる」の意味。

09 feel for someone
動 句 インフォーマル 同情する

I feel for you, I really do. You have the hardest job at the moment.

同情するよ、ほんとうに。あなたが、いま一番きつい仕事をしている。

 I feel for you. で、「お気の毒に」「お察しします」の意味でよく使われる。

Let's Review

07 Sometimes I get _____ with everything. I just want to run away somewhere, someplace where I won't get hurt anymore.

時々、すべてがいやになることがある。どこかに走っていきたい、もう傷つけられることのないどこかに。

08 Focus on yourself, your life and your goals first. Love and the rest will follow; I try to remind myself of this when I _____ about it.

「自分自身、自分の人生、自分の目標にまず集中すること。愛やほかのことは、それについてくるだろう。」落ち込むと、このことを思い出すようにしている。

09 I _____, I really do. You have the hardest job at the moment.

同情するよ、ほんとうに。あなたが、いま一番きつい仕事をしている。

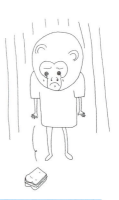

解答 **07** fed up　**08** feel down　**09** feel for someone

DAY 15

10 feet of clay
名 句　不安定な土台、思わぬ欠点

I can tolerate people with feet of clay. What I can't abide are smirking, self-righteous liars.

思わぬ欠点のある人には耐えられる。がまんできないのは、うすら笑いを浮かべる、ひとりよがりのうそつきだ。

▶▶ 体は真鍮でも足元が土でできた彫像が、風で崩れたことから（聖書より）、思わぬ弱点を持つことを「粘土の足」と表した。

11 filthy rich
形 句　大金持ち

I don't wish to be filthy rich. I just yearn for the ultimate success and comfort in every aspect of my life.

大金持ちになることは望んでいない。人生のあらゆる面において、究極の成功と快適さがほしいだけだ。

▶▶ filthy には「汚い」の意味があるが、この場合はたんに「たくさんある」といういこと。何も悪どいことをして金持ちになったという意味ではない。

12 first come, first served
省略　インフォーマル　先着順、早い者勝ち

I have three copies of the HumanKind's book on hand. First come, first served. Find me after the conference!

手元に HumanKind の本が 3 冊あります。先着順です。会議のあとで私を見つけてください。

▶▶ 副詞的用法なら、on a first-come-first-served basis となる。

Let's Review

10 I can tolerate people with _____. What I can't abide are smirking, self-righteous liars.

思わぬ欠点のある人には耐えられる。がまんできないのは、うすら笑いを浮かべる、ひとりよがりのうそつきだ。

11 I don't wish to be _____. I just yearn for the ultimate success and comfort in every aspect of my life.

大金持ちになることは望んでいない。人生のあらゆる面において、究極の成功と快適さがほしいだけだ。

12 I have three copies of the HumanKind's book on hand. _____. Find me after the conference!

手元に HumanKind の本が 3 冊あります。先着順です。会議のあとで私を見つけてください。

解答 **10** feet of clay　**11** filthy rich　**12** First come, first served

DAY 16

fish out of water
名 句　陸に上がったかっぱ、場違いの人間

Eva did not know anyone in the group and felt like a fish out of water.

エヴァはそのグループで誰のことも知らず、場違いのような気がしていた。

▶▶ 陸に上った河童が居心地が悪いように、相当場違いなことを意味する。

flesh and blood
名　生身の人間、血を分けた子ども

I know a lot of people who would be mad if their babies came out ugly. I don't care because that's my flesh and blood.

自分の赤ん坊が醜いと分かったら気が狂うだろう人をたくさん知っている。僕は、自分の子どもなのだから気にしない。

▶▶ 血や肉を分けたまさに肉親のこと。

flush it
動 句　スラング　失敗する

My son really flushed it in his Japnese History course.

息子は、日本史の科目でほんとうに大失敗をした。

▶▶ flush it in 〜で、「〜に失敗する」となる。

Let's Review

01 Eva did not know anyone in the group and felt like a _____.

エヴァはそのグループで誰のことも知らず、場違いのような気がしていた。

02 I know a lot of people who would be mad if their babies came out ugly. I don't care because that's my _____.

自分の赤ん坊が醜いと分かったら気が狂うだろう人をたくさん知っている。僕は、自分の子どもなのだから気にしない。

03 My son really _____ in his Japnese History course.

息子は、日本史の科目でほんとうに大失敗をした。

解答 **01** fish out of water **02** flesh and blood **03** flushed it

DAY 16

04 flying high
形 スラング とてもうれしい、有頂天

Lionel Messi was flying high after his team won the game.
リオネル・メッシは、チームが試合に勝ったあと、有頂天になった。

▶▶ fly high は「高く飛ぶ、高望みする、大志を抱く」。有頂天は通例 (be) flying high となる。

05 fly in the ointment
名 句 インフォーマル 玉にきず、(楽しみの)ぶち壊し

Mark and Julia had a lot of fun at the beach in Hawaii. The only fly in the ointment was Mark's cutting his foot on a piece of glass.
マークとジュリアは、ハワイのビーチでとても楽しんだ。唯一の問題は、ガラスの破片でマークが足を切ったことだった。

▶▶ よく効く薬 (ointment) にハエ (fly) が入っていて薬が台無しになったという聖書の話から、小さなことがすべてを台無しにすることを表す。

06 fly the coop
動 句 スラング 脱走する、逃げる

I want to see my friends and need to fly the coop ASAP.
僕は友人に会いたい、そしてできるだけ早く逃げ出す必要がある。

▶▶「苦境にたって逃げ出す」のほかに、「大人になって親元(狭い鶏小屋)を離れる」の意味もある。

Let's Review

04 Lionel Messi was _____ after his team won the game.

リオネル・メッシは、チームが試合に勝ったあと、有頂天になった。

05 Mark and Julia had a lot of fun at the beach in Hawaii. The only _____ was Mark's cutting his foot on a piece of glass.

マークとジュリアは、ハワイのビーチでとても楽しんだ。唯一の問題は、ガラスの破片でマークが足を切ったことだった。

06 I want to see my friends and need to _____ ASAP.

僕は友人に会いたい、そしてできるだけ早く逃げ出す必要がある。

解答 **04** flying high   **05** fly in the ointment   **06** fly the coop

DAY 16

07 food for thought
名 句 考える材料

Julia gave Eva food for thought on this topic.

ジュリアはこの話題についてエヴァに考える材料を与えた。

▶▶ The book gave me food for thought. とすれば、「本を読んで考えさせられた」となる。

---

08 fool around
動 インフォーマル あてもなくぶらつく、気まぐれに行う

I don't wanna fool around and make a mistake again. Time is of the essence and I have none to waste.

僕は気まぐれに進めてまた失敗したくない。時間がきわめて重要であり、むだにしているひまはない。

▶▶ fool about も同義で使われる。しばしば否定形でも使用される。Don't fool around.「ぶらぶらするな」

---

09 foot in the door
名 句 インフォーマル 最初の一歩を踏み出す

Need experience? Internships may help you get your foot in the door.

経験が必要ですか？ インターンシップが、最初の一歩を踏み出す助けになるかもしれません。

▶▶ get one's foot in the door of ～で、「～への足掛かりをつかむ」。

Let's Review

07 Julia gave Eva _____ on this topic.

ジュリアはこの話題についてエヴァに考える材料を与えた。

08 I don't wanna _____ and make a mistake again. Time is of the essence and I have none to waste.

僕は気まぐれに進めてまた失敗したくない。時間がきわめて重要であり、むだにしているひまはない。

09 Need experience? Internships may help you get your _____.

経験が必要ですか？ インターンシップが、最初の一歩を踏み出す助けになるかもしれません。

解答　**07** food for thought　**08** fool around　**09** foot in the door

DAY 16

10 for all I know
副句 私が知る限りでは

For all I know, Mark may have left town.
私が知る限りでは、マークは街を出たかもしれない。

▶▶ よくは知らないが、私の持っている情報をすべて考え合わせると、
のニュアンスが含まれる。

---

11 for days on end
副句 何日もずっと

Cristiano Ronaldo is enjoying allowing his phone to die and making no effort to charge it for days on end.
クリスティアーノ・ロナウドは、バッテリーが切れるまで電話を使うのを楽しみ、何日間も充電しようとしていない。

▶▶ on end に「立て続けに」の意味がある。Doctor, I've had this pain days on end.「先生、この痛みがずっと続いているんです」

---

12 for dear life
副句 必死で

She was holding on to the seat belt for dear life.
彼女は必死でシートベルトにしがみついていた。

▶▶ dear には「大事な、貴重な」という意味がある。for one's life と同義。

Let's Review

10 _____, Mark may have left town.

私が知る限りでは、マークは街を出たかもしれない。

11 Cristiano Ronaldo is enjoying allowing his phone to die and making no effort to charge it _____.

クリスティアーノ・ロナウドは、バッテリーが切れるまで電話を使うのを楽しみ、何日間も充電しようとしていない。

12 She was holding on to the seat belt _____.

彼女は必死でシートベルトにしがみついていた。

解答 **10** For all I know **11** for days on end **12** for dear life

DAY 17

01 fork over
動句 差しだす、支払う

He just forked over $200 in taxes to the federal government.
彼は連邦政府に 200 ドルの税金を支払ったばかりだ。

▶▶ fork over … for ～の形で使われることが多い。

02 for sure
副句 確かに

No one knows for sure when exactly The Ice Bucket Challenge started.
アイス・バケツ・チャレンジが正確にいつ始まったのか、誰も確かなことは知らない。

▶▶ 会話で返事に For sure. と言うと、「はい」「もちろん」の意味になる。

03 for the better
形 副 句 より良い状態に向かって

I am growing and changing for the better.
僕は成長し、より良い状態に向かって変わりつつある。

▶▶ 動詞 change といっしょに使うことで、良い方向に変化しているイメージとなる。

Let's Review

01 He just _____ $200 in taxes to the federal government.

彼は連邦政府に 200 ドルの税金を支払ったばかりだ。

02 No one knows _____ when exactly The Ice Bucket Challenge started.

アイス・バケツ・チャレンジが正確にいつ始まったのか、誰も確かなことは知らない。

03 I am growing and changing _____.

僕は成長し、より良い状態に向かって変わりつつある。

解答 **01** forked over **02** for sure **03** for the better

DAY 17

freak out
動句 スラング 怖がらせる、動揺する

We had the power turned off last night for a few hours and I was freaked out.

昨夜は電気が数時間止まり、僕は動揺した。

▶▶ to panic、to lose control などに意味は近い。Don't freak out! で、「落ち着いて！」の意味。

---

free rein
名 行動の自由、自由裁量

I have been given free rein to go and buy a computer at Best Buy. This is too much responsibility!

僕はベスト・バイに行って、好きなようにコンピューターを買う自由を与えられた。これは責任が大きすぎるよ！

▶▶ give free rein の後は to 不定詞が来て、「〜する自由を与える」となる。

---

from scratch
副句 インフォーマル 最初から

It's been difficult adjusting to a whole new world, where I practically don't know anybody and must start from scratch.

まったく新しい世界に適応するのは難しかった。そこではほとんど誰も知らず、初めからスタートしなければならないのだ。

▶▶ scratch は、引っかいて描いた最初の線という意味があり、転じて「最初から」「ゼロから」となった。

Let's Review

04 We had the power turned off last night for a few hours and I was _____.

昨夜は電気が数時間止まり、僕は動揺した。

05 I have been given _____ to go and buy a computer at Best Buy. This is too much responsibility!

僕はベスト・バイに行って、好きなようにコンピューターを買う自由を与えられた。これは責任が大きすぎるよ！

06 It's been difficult adjusting to a whole new world, where I practically don't know anybody and must start _____.

まったく新しい世界に適応するのは難しかった。そこではほとんど誰も知らず、初めからスタートしなければならないのだ。

解答 **04** freaked out **05** free rein **06** from scratch

DAY 17

 from the heart

副 心の底から

Gift giving should be from the heart and not from the wallet.

ギフトは、お金ではなく心を込めて贈るべきです。

▶▶ sincerely, honestly と同義。

---

 from time to time

副 句 時々

Julia tries new recipes from time to time, but Mark never likes them.

ジュリアは時々新しいレシピを試しているが、マークは決してそれが好きではない。

▶▶ from A to A は、そのうちのある A から別の A まで、順不同にまたは不定期に見ていっている感じ。

---

 fuddy-duddy

名 時代遅れの

Eva always thinks Mark is an old fuddy-duddy.

エヴァは常に、マークが古くさくて時代遅れの人間だと考えている。

▶▶ 見た目だけではなく態度が古臭いような場合にも用いる。複数形は fuddy-duddies。

Let's Review

07 Gift giving should be _____ and not from the wallet.

ギフトは、お金ではなく心を込めて贈るべきです。

08 Julia tries new recipes _____, but Mark never likes them.

ジュリアは時々新しいレシピを試しているが、マークは決してそれが好きではない。

09 Eva always thinks Mark is an old _____.

エヴァは常に、マークが古くさくて時代遅れの人間だと考えている。

解答　**07** from the heart　**08** from time to time　**09** fuddy-duddy

DAY 17

10 full-bodied
形 力強い、こくのある

If you love full-bodied wine, prepare to fall in love!
こくのあるワインが大好きなら、恋に落ちる準備をしなさい。

▶▶ ワインの味わいを表すときに頻繁に使用する。

---

11 full-fledged
形 成熟した、本格的な

Strangely, even a month after Bill Gates ordered, the web-designer doesn't have a full-fledged website.
奇妙なことに、ビル・ゲイツが命じた 1 か月後になっても、そのウェブデザイナーは本格的なウェブサイトを持っていない。

▶▶ fledge で、「羽毛が生え揃ったヒナ」の意味がある。

---

12 game is up or jig is up
策略がばれる、万事休す

The jig is up. Mark knows Eva has been smoking in the basement.
万事休す。マークは、エヴァが地下でタバコを吸っていることを知っている。

▶▶ jig とは、テンポの速いダンスのこと。in jig time で「敏速に」、jig about で「そわそわする」という慣用句もある。

Let's Review

10 If you love _____ wine, prepare to fall in love!

こくのあるワインが大好きなら、恋に落ちる準備をしなさい。

11 Strangely, even a month after Bill Gates ordered, the web-designer doesn't have a _____ website.

奇妙なことに、ビル・ゲイツが命じた1か月後になっても、そのウェブデザイナーは本格的なウェブサイトを持っていない。

12 The _____. Mark knows Eva has been smoking in the basement.

万事休す。マークは、エヴァが地下でタバコを吸っていることを知っている。

解答 **10** full-bodied **11** full-fledged **12** jig is up

01 gee whiz
間 インフォーマル うわー、おいおい

Gee whiz! My thighs are burning.
うわあ。両方の太ももがひりひりする。

▶▶ 会話では、gee だけで「おや！ まあ！ 驚いた！」の意味で用いる。

---

02 get across
動 〜を理解させる

He is not very good at getting his ideas across.
彼は自分の考えを理解させるのがあまり上手くない。

▶▶ 「横切って向こう側に行く」から転じて、相手を「理解させる」となった。

---

03 get a grip on
動 句 〜を理解する、把握する

How do I stop all these thoughts? I need to get a grip on myself.
こういうすべての考えを、どうやったら止められるの？ 自分自身をしっかり把握する必要があるわ。

▶▶ 感情面、行動面の両方について自制することをいう。

Let's Review

01 _____ !
My thighs are burning.

うわあ。両方の太ももがひりひりする。

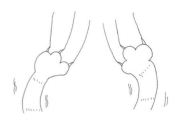

02 He is not very good at _____.

彼は自分の考えを理解させるのがあまり上手くない。

03 How do I stop all these thoughts? I need to _____ myself.

こういうすべての考えを、どうやったら止められるの？ 自分自身をしっかり把握する必要があるわ。

解答 **01** Gee whiz **02** getting his ideas across **03** get a grip on

DAY 18

04 get a kick out of
動　句　〜を面白がる

John Lennon gets a kick out of walking really slowly across the road to make impatient drivers wait.

ジョン・レノンは実にゆっくりと歩いて道路を渡り、イライラしている運転手を待たせることを面白がっている。

▶▶ kick に「麻薬から得る興奮」の意味があることから転じた表現。

---

05 get a rise out of
動　句　スラング　〜を怒らせる、むきにならせる

Messi gets a rise out of Ronaldo by teasing him about his fashion.

メッシはロナルドのファッションをからかうことで、彼を怒らせる。

▶▶ of の後には、人が来ること。

---

06 get back at
動　インフォーマル　仕返しをする

Alice had an affair to get back at her cheating husband.

アリスは不倫をして、浮気している夫に仕返しをした。

▶▶ revenge「復しゅうする」よりは軽いイメージで使える。

Let's Review

04 John Lennon _____ walking really slowly across the road to make impatient drivers wait.

ジョン・レノンは実にゆっくりと歩いて道路を渡り、イライラしている運転手を待たせることを面白がっている。

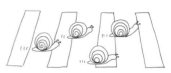

05 Messi _____ Ronaldo by teasing him about his fashion.

メッシはロナルドのファッションをからかうことで、彼を怒らせる。

06 Alice had an affair to _____ her cheating husband.

アリスは不倫をして、浮気している夫に仕返しをした。

解答 **04** gets a kick out of **05** gets a rise out of **06** get back at

DAY 18

07 get behind
動 遅れをとる

If you don't check your E-mail regularly, you'll get behind at your work.

定期的にEメールをチェックしなければ、仕事で遅れをとることになるだろう。

▶▶ get behind ～には「～を後援［支持］する」という意味もある。

08 get by
動 インフォーマル どうにかやっていく

Alberto can just about get by in Korean.

アルベルトは、韓国語でほとんどどうにかやっていくことができる。

▶▶「うまくやって行く」であれば、get by fine ～となる。

09 get going
動 インフォーマル 活動を開始する、取りかかる

Julia needs some type of motivation to get her going.

ジュリアは活動を開始するために、ある種の動機付けを必要としている。

▶▶ When the going gets tough, the tough get going.「事態が困難になるとタフな人たちが動き出す」《諺》

Let's Review

07 If you don't check your E-mail regularly, you'll _____ at your work.

定期的にEメールをチェックしなければ、仕事で遅れをとることになるだろう。

08 Alberto can just about _____ in Korean.

アルベルトは、韓国語でほとんどどうにかやっていくことができる。

09 Julia needs some type of motivation to _____.

ジュリアは活動を開始するために、ある種の動機付けを必要としている。

解答　**07** get behind　**08** get by　**09** get her going

DAY 18

10 get off one's back
動 スラング 会話 邪魔をしない

Get off my back. I don't live for you.
邪魔をしないで。あなたのために生きているわけじゃない。

▶▶ Leave me alone! と似た表現となる。

---

11 get on one's case
動 句 うるさく口を出す、干渉する

It is amazing how girls I once dated **get on my case** for not approaching them about having a serious relationship.
かつてデートした女の子たちが、真剣につきあおうと僕が彼女たちに迫らないことで、うるさく口を出してくるとは驚きだ。

▶▶ Why do you keep getting on my case?「どうして私のことに干渉し続けるのか？」

---

12 get real
動 句 インフォーマル 現実に目を向ける

Get real Mark, you'll never win the lottery.
現実を見なさい、マーク。あなたは決して宝くじに当たることはない。

▶▶ 宝くじに当たることや有名女優と付き合うといったありそうもないことを夢想しているような人に対して使うことが多い。

Let's Review

10 _____. I don't live for you.

邪魔をしないで。あなたのために生きているわけじゃない。

11 It is amazing how girls I once dated _____ for not approaching them about having a serious relationship.

かつてデートした女の子たちが、真剣に付き合おうと彼女たちに迫らないことで、うるさく口を出してくるとは驚きだ。

12 _____ Mark, you'll never win the lottery.

現実を見なさい、マーク。あなたは決して宝くじに当たることはない。

解答 **10** Get off my back　**11** get on my case　**12** Get real

DAY 19

01 get the eye
動 句　インフォーマル　❶熱い視線を浴びる

Upton got the eye as she walked past the boys on the street.　アプトンは、道で男の子たちの前を歩いて通りすぎていくと、熱い視線を浴びた。

❷冷たい目で見る

When Julia asked if she could take home the laundry and pay later, she got the eye from the clerk.

ジュリアが洗濯物を家に持ち帰り、後で支払うことができるかと尋ねると、店員から冷たい目で見られた。

▶▶「視線を得る」から派生して、「色目を使われる」という意味もある。

02 get the sack
動 句　スラング　クビになる

Alice got the sack at the company yesterday.
アリスは昨日、会社をクビになった。

Eva gave Mark the sack.　エヴァはマークを解雇した。

▶▶クビにするときに身の回りの品を入れるための袋（sack）を渡したことが由来と言われている。

03 get under one's skin
動 句　(人を)ひどく怒らせる

Julia really knows how to get under Mark's skin just by talking.

ジュリアは、ただ話をするだけでマークをひどく怒らせる方法を実によく知っている。

▶▶「(人)の心を強く捕らえる、(人)を魅了する、とりこにする」という意味もある。

Let's Review

01 When Julia asked if she could take home the laundry and pay later, she _____ from the clerk.

ジュリアが洗濯物を家に持ち帰り、後で支払うことができるかと尋ねると、店員から冷たい目で見られた。

02 Alice _____ at the company yesterday.

アリスは昨日、会社をクビになった。

03 Julia really knows how to _____ just by talking.

ジュリアは、ただ話をするだけでマークをひどく怒らせる方法を実によく知っている。

解答 **01** got the eye **02** got the sack **03** get under Mark's skin

DAY 19

04 get up on the wrong side of the bed

機嫌が悪い

Definitely Eva got up on the wrong side of the bed today.

エヴァは今日、確かに機嫌が悪い。

▶▶ get up の代わりに wake up でもよい。

---

05 get with it

動 句 スラング 身を入れてやる

The professor told the students to get with it.

教授は学生たちに、身を入れてやるように話した。

▶▶ 流行に遅れないようにというときは、New style is in, so get with it.「新しいスタイルが流行っているから、遅れないように！」

---

06 give it to one straight

動 句 率直に物を言う

I don't wanna be in love alone. So give it to me straight.

片思いをするのは嫌い。だからはっきり言ってほしいの。

▶▶ Give it to me straight, doctor. Have I got cancer?「先生、正直に言ってください。私は癌ですか？」

Let's Review

04 Definitely Eva _____ today.

エヴァは今日、確かに機嫌が悪い。

05 The professor told the students to _____.

教授は学生たちに、身を入れてやるように話した。

06 I don't wanna be in love alone. So _____.

片思いをするのは嫌い。だからはっきり言ってほしいの。

解答 **04** got up on the wrong side of the bed **05** get with it
06 give it to me straight

DAY 19

07 give no quarter
動句 情け容赦なく〜する

The machine was created to be giving no quarters to its targets.
その機械は、標的に対して情け容赦をしないように作られた。

▶▶ quarter には「慈悲、容赦」という意味がある。

08 give up the ghost
動句 死ぬ、故障する

My iPhone is about to give up the ghost.
僕の iPhone は故障しかけている。

After a long illness, the old man gave up the ghost.
長い患いの後、その老人は亡くなった。

▶▶「お陀仏した」「お釈迦になった」という日本語に近いかもしれない。

09 go after
動 〜を追い求める

If you really want something in life you should go after it. No matter how hard the struggles are to get what you want.
もし本当に人生で何かを得たいなら、それを追い求めるべきだ。欲しいものを得るために、それがどれほど大変な努力であったとしても。

▶▶ 追いかける (go after) ものは、人・物・事などがくる。

Let's Review

07 The machine was created to be _____ to its targets.

その機械は、標的に対して情け容赦をしないように作られた。

08 My iPhone is about to _____.

僕のiPhoneは故障しかけている。

09 If you really want something in life you should _____ it. No matter how hard the struggles are to get what you want.

もし本当に人生で何かを得たいなら、それを追い求めるべきだ。欲しいものを得るために、それがどれほど大変な努力であったとしても。

解答　**07** giving no quarters　**08** give up the ghost　**09** go after

DAY 19

⑩ go astray
動 句 行方不明になる

Brian's letters went astray or were not delivered.
ブライアンの手紙は行方不明になったか、または配達されていない。

▶▶ lead (someone) astray で、「~を迷わせる、だます」となる。astray は形容詞で「道に迷って／道を踏みはずして」の意味。

⑪ gobble up
動 句 食べつくす

Can you catch all of the ants before they gobble up my sandwiches?
アリが僕のサンドイッチを食べつくす前に、全部捕まえてくれる？

▶▶ 時間をかけずに、素早く完全に食べるというニュアンスが含まれる。

⑫ go Dutch
動 句 インフォーマル 割り勘

Julia knew Mansour had little money, so she offered to go Dutch.
ジュリアは、マンスールがほとんどお金を持っていないことを知っていたので、割り勘を申し出た。

▶▶ Let's go fifty-fifty. Let's split. としても同義となる。

Let's Review

10 Brian's letters _____ or were not delivered.

ブライアンの手紙は行方不明になったか、または配達されていない。

11 Can you catch all of the ants before they _____ my sandwiches?

アリが僕のサンドイッチを食べつくす前に、全部捕まえてくれる？

12 Julia knew Mansour had little money, so she offered to _____.

ジュリアは、マンスールがほとんどお金を持っていないことを知っていたので、割り勘を申し出た。

解答　**10** went astray　**11** gobble up　**12** go Dutch

DAY 20

01 go-getter
名 やり手、凄腕

Brian is a go-getter. He doesn't stop until he gets what he wants.
ブライアンは凄腕だ。欲しい物を手に入れるまで立ち止まらない。

▶▶ 早々と出世していく人のこともいう。

---

02 going on
形 句 〜に近づいている、ほぼ

It is going on eight o'clock.
8時に近づいている。

Mark is going on 30 years old.
マークは30歳くらいだ。

▶▶ 何かが始まっていて、そのまま進行中であることを指す。

---

03 good egg
名 句 インフォーマル 信頼できる人

A true friend is one who thinks you are a good egg even if you are half-cracked.
真の友とは、あなたが少しおかしいとしても、信頼できると思ってくれる人だ。

▶▶ 反意語は、bad egg で良い。

Let's Review

01 Brian is a _____.
He doesn't stop until he gets what he wants.

ブライアンは凄腕だ。欲しい物を手に入れるまで立ち止まらない。

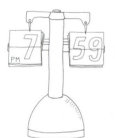

02 It is _____ eight o'clock.

8時に近づいている。

03 A true friend is one who thinks you are a _____ even if you are half-cracked.

真の友とは、あなたが少しおかしいとしても、信頼できると思ってくれる人だ。

解答 **01** go-getter **02** going on **03** good egg

DAY 20

04 good-for-nothing
形 句 ろくでなし

While Alice studies hard each day, her good-for-nothing boyfriend hangs around in the bars.

アリスが毎日一生懸命勉強している一方で、ろくでなしのボーイフレンドはバーをうろついている。

▶▶ useless とほぼ同義で形容詞的に使える。

05 goof off
動 スラング さぼる、怠ける

It is amazing how Tyler goofed off all week in class and ended up with a better score than everyone in the class.

授業を丸1週間さぼったタイラーが、最終的にクラスの誰よりもいい点を取ったのは驚きだ。

▶▶ I'm no goof-off.「私は怠け者ではない」など、goof-off で名詞として使える。

06 go steady
動 句 きまった異性と交際する、ステディである

Julia's parents met in high school, and they went steady for 8 years before finally getting married.

ジュリアの両親は高校で出会い、8年間交際してからついに結婚した。

▶▶ 決まった一人と交際することを意味し、そこから「まじめに(着実に)やる」という意味もある。

Let's Review

04 While Alice studies hard each day, her _____ boyfriend hangs around in the bars.

アリスが毎日一生懸命勉強している一方で、ろくでなしのボーイフレンドはバーをうろついている。

05 It is amazing how Tyler _____ all week in class and ended up with a better score than everyone in the class.

授業を丸1週間さぼったタイラーが、最終的にクラスの誰よりもいい点を取ったのは驚きだ。

06 Julia's parents met in high school, and they _____ for 8 years before finally getting married.

ジュリアの両親は高校で出会い、8年間交際してからついに結婚した。

解答 **04** good-for-nothing **05** goofed off **06** went steady

DAY 20

07 go straight
動 句 スラング 更生する、まっとうな生活を送る

After the man got out of prison, he went straight.

その男は刑務所から出た後、まっとうな生活を送っている。

▶▶「まっすぐに行く」であれば、go straight ahead とすると意味が明確になる。

---

08 go wrong
動 句 失敗する

Life is short. So don't worry about where you went wrong.

人生は短い。だから過去に失敗した時のことで悩むな。

▶▶ can't go wrong で「必ずうまくいく」。

---

09 green with envy
形 句 ひどくうらやんで

I'm not a jealous person normally. But at this moment I'm green with envy. I want to go on holidays today.

私はふだん、人をねたむ人間ではない。けれどいまは、うらやましくてたまらない。今日、休暇旅行に出かけたい。

▶▶ 妬みすぎて、顔色まで青くなることから。例文にある go on holiday は「休暇ででかける（旅行する）」の慣用表現。

Let's Review

07 After the man got out of prison,
he _____.

その男は刑務所から出た後、まっとうな生活を送っている。

08 Life is short. So don't worry about where you _____.

人生は短い。だから過去に失敗した時のことで悩むな。

09 I'm not a jealous person normally. But at this moment
I'm _____.
I want to go on holidays today.

私はふだん、人をねたむ人間ではない。けれどいまは、うらやましくてたまらない。今日、休暇旅行に出かけたい。

解答 **07** went straight　**08** went wrong　**09** green with envy

DAY 20

10 grin and bear it
動句 耐える

There's nothing we can do about it. We'll just have to grin and bear it.
私たちにできることは何もない。ひたすら耐えていかなきゃならないのね。

▶▶ もとは、船乗りが長い悪天候を憂いて使った表現とされる。

11 gung-ho
形 会話 献身的な、任務を熱心に遂行する

She has no musical talent, I don't understand why the label is gung-ho on making her the singer.
彼女には音楽の才能がない。彼女を歌手にすることについて、なぜレーベルが熱心に売り出すのかまったく理解できない。

▶▶ 〜についてと続ける場合の前置詞は、on を用いる。

12 had better
インフォーマル 〜した方がいい

We had better leave now or we'll miss the plane.
僕たちはすぐに出発した方がいい、でないと飛行機に乗り遅れるだろう。

▶▶ よく使う表現だが、もしそうしないと大変な結果になることを暗示しているので、「必ず〜した方がいい」と覚えよう。社会的に立場の上の人にはあまり使わない。

Let's Review

10 There's nothing we can do about it. We'll just have to _____.

私たちにできることは何もない。ひたすら耐えていかなきゃならないのね。

11 She has no musical talent, I don't understand why the label is _____ on making her the singer.

彼女には音楽の才能がない。彼女を歌手にすることについて、なぜレーベルが熱心に売り出すのかまったく理解できない。

12 We _____ leave now or we'll miss the plane.

僕たちはすぐに出発した方がいい、でないと飛行機に乗り遅れるだろう。

解答 **10** grin and bear it **11** gung-ho **12** had better

DAY 21

01 hand over fist

形 インフォーマル たやすく、急速に

Brian and David are making money hand over fist.

ブライアンとデイヴィッドは、濡れ手に粟で金を儲けている。

▶▶ make money hand over fist で「ぼろ儲けする」とひとつの慣用表現となる。

---

02 hands down

形 句 ❶ 楽々と

Giants won the game hands down.

ジャイアンツは、楽々と試合に勝った。

❷ 確実な、間違いのない

Show Me The Money is the best show! Hands down!

ショウ・ミー・ザ・マネーは最高のショーだ！間違いないね。

▶▶ 競馬の騎手が手を下げたまま（hands down）でもレースに勝てたことからきた表現。

---

03 hangover

名 二日酔い

Julia woke up with a terrible hangover.

ジュリアはひどい二日酔いで目が覚めた。

▶▶ 酒だけでなく、薬が残って具合が悪いほか過去の遺物、後遺症、余波の意味もある。

Let's Review

01 Brian and David are making money _____.

プライアンとデイヴィッドは、濡れ手に粟で金を儲けている。

02 Giants won the game _____.

ジャイアンツは、楽々と試合に勝った。

03 Julia woke up with a terrible _____.

ジュリアはひどい二日酔いで目が覚めた。

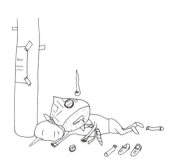

解答 **01** hand over fist　**02** hands down　**03** hangover

DAY 21

04 happy camper
名 **インフォーマル** ご機嫌な人、楽しんでいる人

Ophelia is not a happy camper because of what she heard about her husband.
オフィーリアは、夫について耳にしたことのために楽しんでいない。

▶▶ camp「キャンプ」はとても楽しいこととされているため。

---

05 hardheaded
形 頭が固い

Some artists gotta go learn how to write a song. Failure is guaranteed when they got a big ego and hardheaded.
アーティストの中には、歌の作り方を習いにいかねばならなかった者もいる。うぬぼれが強くて頭が固いと、まちがいなく失敗する。

▶▶ soft-headed は「ばかな、頭の悪い」。

---

06 hard line
名 **句** 強硬路線

Singaporean government took a hard line on drug dealers.
シンガポール政府は、麻薬の密売人に対して強硬路線を取った。

▶▶ 反意語は soft line「柔軟路線」。

Let's Review

04 Ophelia is not a _____ because of what she heard about her husband.

オフィーリアは、夫について耳にしたことのために楽しんでいない。

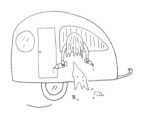

05 Some artists gotta go learn how to write a song. Failure is guaranteed when they got a big ego and _____.

アーティストの中には、歌の作り方を習いにいかねばならなかった者もいる。うぬぼれが強くて頭が固いと、まちがいなく失敗する。

06 Singaporean government took a _____ on drug dealers.

シンガポール政府は、麻薬の密売人に対して強硬路線を取った。

解答 **04** happy camper **05** hardheaded **06** hard line

07 **have an eye for**
動 句 〜を見る目がある

Girls talk to each other like men talk to each other. But girls have an eye for detail.

女の子同士は、男性同士が互いに話すように話す。しかし女の子たちには、細部を見る目があるのだ。

▶▶ have an ear for 〜は「〜を聞く耳がある、〜に対して耳が肥えている、〜を理解できる」という表現。

08 **have got to**
動 句 〜しなければならない

Julia has got to break this bad habit of eating in bed.

ジュリアは、ベッドの中で物を食べる悪い習慣を止めなければならない。

▶▶ 日本の英語の授業で取り上げられることはめったにないが、実際の会話では多くの人が使っている表現。

09 **have in mind**
動 句 〜を考える

I have in mind what I want to wear for my cousin's wedding.

私は、いとこの結婚式に何が着たいかと考えている。

▶▶ 「mind」の前には「a、the、your」などの単語はつかない。

Let's Review

07 Girls talk to each other like men talk to each other. But girls _____ detail.

女の子同士は、男性同士が互いに話すように話す。しかし女の子たちには、細部を見る目があるのだ。

08 Julia _____ break this bad habit of eating in bed.

ジュリアは、ベッドの中で物を食べる悪い習慣を止めなければならない。

09 I _____ what I want to wear for my cousin's wedding.

私は、いとこの結婚式に何が着たいかと考えている。

解答 **07** have an eye for   **08** has got to   **09** have in mind

⑩ have it coming

動 句 自業自得である

I feel sorry about Alice's failing that course, but she had it coming to her.

アリスがその科目を落としたのは残念に思うけれど、自業自得だね。

▶▶ 〜 it coming を使った表現：How's it coming?「例の件どうなってる？」、Keep it coming.「どんどん頼むよ［持ってきて］」、see it coming「それが起こりそうな気配を感じる」

⑪ have one's cake and eat it too

動 句 両立させる、一挙両得

Mark had been playing double. Looks like he was trying to have his cake and eat it too.

マークは両方にいい顔をしていた。一挙両得を狙っていたようだ。

▶▶ You can't have your cake and eat it too.「ケーキを食べたらケーキを持っていることはできない（ケーキは食べたらなくなる）」《諺》より。

⑫ have the last laugh

動 句 最後に笑う

We'll see who is the one who has the last laugh.

誰が最後に笑うのかがわかるだろう。

▶▶ He laughs best who laughs last.「最後に笑う者が最もよく笑う」《諺》から影響を受けた表現。

Let's Review

10 I feel sorry about Alice's failing that course, but she _____ to her.

アリスがその科目を落としたのは残念に思うけれど、自業自得だね。

11 Mark had been playing double. Looks like he was trying to

_____.

マークは両方にいい顔をしていた。一挙両得を狙っていたようだ。

12 We'll see who is the one who _____.

誰が最後に笑うのかがわかるだろう。

解答 **10** had it coming **11** have his cake and eat it too **12** has the last laugh

DAY 22

01 hell and high water
名 句 たいへんな苦境

My friend has gone through hell and high water to be a leading businessman. I hope he makes it.

友人は、優れたビジネスマンになるためにたいへんな苦境を経験した。彼がうまくいくといいなあ。

▶▶ 直訳すると「地獄と洪水」。

02 hem and haw
動 句 口ごもる

Mark hemmed and hawed, but finally told Julia the truth.

マークは口ごもっていたが、とうとうジュリアに本当のことを話した。

▶▶ hem「口ごもる」、haw「えー、と口ごもる」。

03 hit-and-run
形 ひき逃げする

Julia just saw a hit-and-run on the street about 30 minutes ago.

ジュリアは約30分前、路上でのひき逃げをちょうど目撃した。

▶▶ 野球起源の句で「ヒット・エンド・ラン」に由来する。

Let's Review

01 My friend has gone through _____ to be a leading businessman. I hope he makes it.

友人は、優れたビジネスマンになるためにたいへんな苦境を経験した。彼がうまくいくといいなあ。

02 Mark _____, but finally told Julia the truth.

マークは口ごもっていたが、とうとうジュリアに本当のことを話した。

03 Julia just saw a _____ on the street about 30 minutes ago.

ジュリアは約 30 分前、路上でのひき逃げをちょうど目撃した。

解答 **01** hell and high water **02** hemmed and hawed **03** hit-and-run

DAY 22

hit a nerve
動 句 〜の神経にさわることを言う

When Mark called Eva a retarded woman, the remark hit a nerve so strongly that she gave him a slap in the face.

マークがエヴァを知恵の遅れた女と呼んだとき、この言葉があまりにも神経にさわったので、彼女は彼の顔を平手打ちした。

▶▶ hit/touch a raw nerve とも言う。

---

hit home
動 句 胸にしみる

I learned in class today that "It's not the person, it's what you think of the person." That hit home, you have to find the good in someone.

今日授業で、「問題はその人ではなく、あなたがその人のことをどう考えるかだ」と習った。これは胸にしみた、あなたは人の良い点を探さなければならないのだ。

▶▶ ネガティブ「痛いところをつく」にもポジティブ「グッとくる」にも、どちらでも使える。

---

hit it off
動 句 インフォーマル 仲よくやる

Brian and Alice really hit it off tonight.

ブライアンとアリスは、今夜は本当に仲よくやっている。

▶▶ get along (with) と同義。

Let's Review

04 When Mark called Eva a retarded woman, the remark _____ so strongly that she gave him a slap in the face.

マークがエヴァを知恵の遅れた女と呼んだとき、この言葉があまりにも神経にさわったので、彼女は彼の顔を平手打ちした。

05 I learned in class today that "It's not the person, it's what you think of the person." That _____, you have to find the good in someone.

今日授業で、「問題はその人ではなく、あなたがその人のことをどう考えるかだ」と習った。これは胸にしみた、あなたは人の良い点を探さなければならないのだ。

06 Brian and Alice really _____ tonight.

ブライアンとアリスは、今夜は本当に仲よくやっている。

解答 **04** hit a nerve　**05** hit home　**06** hit it off

DAY 22

07 hit the ceiling
動 句 スラング かんしゃくを起こす

When Casanova cheated on his wife, she hit the ceiling.
カサノヴァが妻を裏切ったとき、彼女はかんしゃくを起こした。

▶▶ 数多くの同義語がある：flip one's lid, flip one's wig, fly off the handle, go ballistic, have a fit, have kittens, hit the roof, lose one's temper, throw a fit, blow a fuse, blow one's stack, blow up, combust

08 hit the hay
動 句 スラング 寝る

Alright dude, I am gonna hit the hay! Good night!
よーし、寝よう。おやすみ！

▶▶ hit the sack と同義。

09 hit the road
動 句 スラング 出かける

I am gonna go to take a bath and get ready to hit the road for New York in a few minutes.
風呂にはいったら数分でニューヨークに出かける準備をするよ。

▶▶ hit the trail と同義。

Let's Review

07 When Casanova cheated on his wife, she _____.

カサノヴァが妻を裏切ったとき、彼女はかんしゃくを起こした。

08 Alright dude, I am gonna _____! Good night!

よーし、寝よう。おやすみ！

09 I am gonna go to take a bath and get ready to _____ for New York in a few minutes.

風呂にはいったら数分でニューヨークに出かける準備をするよ。

解答　**07** hit the ceiling　**08** hit the hay　**09** hit the road

DAY 22

⑩ honeymoon is over
蜜月期間は終わり

Barack Obama's honeymoon is over. Congress and the President began to criticize each other.

バラク・オバマの蜜月期間は終わった。連邦議会と大統領は、互いに批判し始めた。

▶▶ 蜜月［幸福な］期間は honeymoon period/stage。

⑪ hooked on
形 ❶ 中毒になっている

Mark is hooked on smoking, but Julia is only hooked on coffee.

マークはタバコ中毒だ。だが、ジュリアはただコーヒー中毒なだけだ。

❷ 〜に夢中である

I never understood how some people get hooked on SNS!

SNSに夢中になっている人がいるなんて、まったく理解できない。

▶▶ be addicted to と同義。

⑫ horse sense
名 インフォーマル 常識

Alvin is well educated and read many books, but still does not have much horse sense.

アルヴィンはきちんと教育を受けて多くの本を読んでいるが、いまだに大した常識を備えていない。

▶▶ 馬は落馬した人を決して蹴らないとか、えさを食べているときは消化に悪いため水を飲まないなどと言われていることから。

Let's Review

10 Barack Obama's _____.
Congress and the President began to criticize each other.

バラク・オバマの蜜月期間は終わった。連邦議会と大統領は、互いに批判し始めた。

11 Mark is _____ smoking, but Julia is only _____ coffee.

マークはタバコ中毒だ。だが、ジュリアはただコーヒー中毒なだけだ。

12 Alvin is well educated and read many books, but still does not have much _____.

アルヴィンはきちんと教育を受けて多くの本を読んでいるが、いまだに大した常識を備えていない。

解答 **10** honeymoon is over **11** hooked on **12** horse sense

DAY 23

01 hot air
名 インフォーマル 自慢話、くだらない話

One of his co-worker is just full of hot air and self-regard.

彼の同僚の一人は自慢話ばかりしていて、うぬぼれている。

▶▶ (be) full of と組み合わせて使う。

---

02 hot potato
名 インフォーマル 難問

The prime minister's resignation has become a political hot potato.

首相の辞職は、政治上の難問となった。

▶▶ 焼いたばかりのじゃがいもは熱くて扱いに苦労することから。

---

03 I couldn't agree with you more
動 句 全く同感で

I couldn't agree with you more, Mark.

マーク、僕も全く同感だ。

▶▶ 「これ以上同意のしようがない＝同感／まったくその通り」というような意味合い。

Let's Review

01 One of his co-worker is just full of _____ and self-regard.

彼の同僚の一人は自慢話ばかりしていて、うぬぼれている。

02 The prime minister's resignation has become a political _____.

首相の辞職は、政治上の難問となった。

03 _____, Mark.

マーク、僕も全く同感だ。

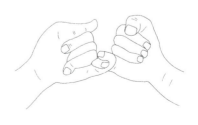

解答 **01** hot air　**02** hot potato　**03** I couldn't agree with you more

DAY 23

04 ill at ease
形 句 不安な、落ち着かない

I can't say as I'm excited about being back in Florida. I feel ill at ease in this state.

フロリダに帰ることに、わくわくしているとは言えない。フロリダ州では不安に感じるのだ。

▶▶ 反意語は at ease「のんびりして、安心して」。

---

05 in a pinch
形 句 インフォーマル いざという時、困った時

In a pinch, light beer can be used to fuel a car.

いざという時には、ライトビールが車の燃料に使える。

▶▶ ここでの意味と関係ないが、PC の再起動などで使うキーコンビネーションコマンド「Ctrl-Alt-Delete」を Vulcan nerve pinch と言う。語源は SF 映画『Star Treck』より。

---

06 in charge of
前 ～担当の

When I get to heaven I'm gonna find the guy in charge of the weather and kick his ass.

天国に行ったら、天気を担当するやつを見つけて叩きのめしたい。

▶▶ charge には「～に委ねる、託す」といった意味もある。

Let's Review

04 I can't say as I'm excited about being back in Florida. I feel _____ in this state.

フロリダに帰ることに、わくわくしているとは言えない。フロリダ州では不安に感じるのだ。

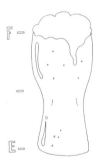

05 _____, light beer can be used to fuel a car.

いざという時には、ライトビールが車の燃料に使える。

06 When I get to heaven I'm gonna find the guy _____ the weather and kick his ass.

天国に行ったら、天気を担当するやつを見つけて叩きのめしたい。

解答 **04** ill at ease **05** In a pinch **06** in charge of

07 in kind
副 句 同じ種類の

Mark returned Eva's insult in kind.

マークはエヴァの侮辱に対して同じやり方で返した。

▶▶ payment in kind「物納、現物払い」が語源。金の代わりに現物で払うところから。

---

08 in one's shoes
副 句 〜の立場で

Have you ever lived my life, have you ever spent one minute in my shoes? If you haven't, then tell me why you judge me like you do.

僕の人生を送ったことがある？ 1分だって僕の立場になったことがある？ そうでなければ、なぜそのように僕を判断するのか聞かせてほしい。

▶▶ fill someone's shoes は「(人)の代役を十分に果たす、後任となる」。

---

09 ins and outs
名 句 〜の詳細、特性

Jobs is learning the ins and outs of Marketing.

ジョブズは、マーケティングの詳細を学んでいるところだ。

▶▶ in and out は「出たり入ったりして、内も外も」。

Let's Review

07 Mark returned Eva's insult _____.

マークはエヴァの侮辱に対して同じやり方で返した。

08 Have you ever lived my life, have you ever spent one minute _____? If you haven't, then tell me why you judge me like you do.

僕の人生を送ったことがある？1分だって僕の立場になったことがある？そうでなければ、なぜそのように僕を判断するのか聞かせてほしい。

09 Jobs is learning the _____ of Marketing.

ジョブズは、マーケティングの詳細を学んでいるところだ。

解答　**07** in kind　**08** in my shoes　**09** ins and outs

DAY 23

10 in the cards
形 句 インフォーマル ありそうな

Two things that will never be in the cards for me: eating whatever I want and having a pimple-free face.

私にとって決してありそうにない２つのこと。好きなものを食べて、吹き出物のない顔でいること。

▶▶ 語源はタロットカードやカード占いから。

11 in the clouds
形 句 うわの空で、空想にふけって

Julia is looking out the window, her head is in the clouds again.

ジュリアは窓の外を眺めている。またしても空想にふけっているのだ。

▶▶ on a cloud は「ウキウキして、この上なく楽しい」、under a cloud は「疑いを掛けられて、塞ぎ込んで」。

12 in the limelight
副 句 人目を引いて、注目されて

Apple Watch is in the limelight of mass communication these days.

Apple Watch はこのところマスコミの注目を浴びている。

▶▶ ライムライト (lime light) は照明器具の一種。電灯が発明され、普及する前に舞台照明に用いられた。別称石灰灯。

Let's Review

10 Two things that will never be _____ for me: eating whatever I want and having a pimple-free face.

私にとって決してありそうにない2つのこと。好きなものを食べて、吹き出物のない顔でいること。

11 Julia is looking out the window, her head is _____ again.

ジュリアは窓の外を眺めている。またしても空想にふけっているのだ。

12 Apple Watch is _____ of mass communication these days.

Apple Watch はこのところマスコミの注目を浴びている。

解答 **10** in the cards **11** in the clouds **12** in the limelight

DAY 24

01 in the red
形 句 インフォーマル 赤字で

My net worth finally dropped in the red.
僕の純資産はついに赤字に転落した。

▶▶ 反意語は in the black「黒字で」。ちなみに in the green は「血気盛んで」、born in the purple だと「王家の家に生まれる」。

02 in the same boat
副 形 句 通常の状態だ

This is normal for now because a lot of people are in the exact same boat.
多くの人々がまったく同じ運命にあるため、いまのところこれが普通の状態だ。

▶▶ 小さな船の乗客が海の上では全員同じリスクを共有することから。

03 into thin air
副 句 見えなくなる、消える

What happened to my Apple devices? They're gone! Disappeared into thin air.
僕の Apple デバイスに何が起こったんだろう？ 全部なくなっちゃった！ 跡形もなく消えちゃった。

▶▶ into the blue と同義。

Let's Review

01 My net worth finally dropped _____.

僕の純資産はついに赤字に転落した。

02 This is normal for now because a lot of people are _____.

多くの人々がまったく同じ運命にあるため、いまのところこれが普通の状態だ。

03 What happened to my Apple devices? They're gone! Disappeared _____.

僕の Apple デバイスに何が起こったんだろう？ 全部なくなっちゃった！ 跡形もなく消えちゃった。

解答 **01** in the red   **02** in the same boat   **03** into thin air

DAY 24

04 in tune
副 形 句 仲よく

Brian is so in tune with Mark when they are together.

ブライアンとマークは、一緒にいる時とても仲がよい。

▶▶ 反意語は out of tune。

---

05 in vain
副 句 むだに

I tried in vain to persuade my son to study.

勉強するよう息子を説得しようとしたが、むだだった。

▶▶ to no avail と同義。

---

06 jawbreaker
名 ❶ 堅いキャンディー

He went to the nearest convenience store to buy some jawbreakers and a chocolate bar.

彼は最寄りのコンビニに行って、堅いキャンディーをいくつかと、チョコレートバーを1本買った。

❷ 発音しにくい語

His name, Gust Avrakotos, is a real jawbreaker.

彼の名前、Gust Avrakotos(ガスト・アヴラコトス)は本当に発音しづらい。

▶▶ jawcrasher「ジョークラッシャー」は破砕機の一種で、垂直に固定された固定ジョーと、一端を固定されながら前後に揺動するスウィングジョーとの間で破砕物を圧砕するもの。

Let's Review

04 Brian is so _____ with Mark when they are together.

ブライアンとマークは、一緒にいる時とても仲がよい。

05 I tried _____ to persuade my son to study.

勉強するよう息子を説得しようとしたが、むだだった。

06 He went to the nearest convenience store to buy some _____ and a chocolate bar.

彼は最寄りのコンビニに行って、堅いキャンディーをいくつかと、チョコレートバーを1本買った。

解答 **04** in tune **05** in vain **06** jawbreaker

DAY 24

07 jump to a conclusion
動 句 早合点する

Julia was asking Brian a question, but before he can finish responding she jumped to a conclusion.
ジュリアはブライアンに質問をしていたが、彼が返答を終える前に、彼女は早合点した。

▶▶ jump the gun は「早まったことをする」。

08 just in case
副 句 万一に備えて

Just in case, David left his phone number.
万一に備えて、デイヴィッドは自分の電話番号を残しておいた。

▶▶ in case ~は「~の場合」という意味。

09 keel over
動 ❶ 転覆する

The strong wind made the boat keel over.
強風でボートが転覆した。

❷ 倒れる
I need food or I may keel over and die.
僕には食べ物が必要だ、じゃないと倒れて死ぬかもしれない。

▶▶ keel は「転覆する、~を転覆させる」という意味。

Let's Review

07 Julia was asking Brian a question, but before he can finish responding she _____.

ジュリアはブライアンに質問をしていたが、彼が返答を終える前に、彼女は早合点した。

08 _____, David left his phone number.

万一に備えて、デイヴィッドは自分の電話番号を残しておいた。

09 The strong wind made the boat _____.

強風でボートが転覆した。

解答 **07** jumped to a conclusion   **08** Just in case   **09** keel over

DAY 24

10 keen about
形 句 〜に夢中で

My girlfriend is very keen to learn about English Idioms.
僕のガールフレンドは、英語のイディオムにすっかり夢中だ。

▶▶ keen on とも言う。

---

11 keep after
動 インフォーマル （〜するように）しつこく言う

She had to keep after Bill Gates to fix the computer.
彼女はビル・ゲイツにコンピュータを修理するようしつこく言わねばならなかった。

▶▶ 「keep after + 人」の形になる。

---

12 keep an eye on
動 句 〜から目を離さないでいる

You always have to keep an eye on your children at all times, when you look away they disappear.
いつでも必ず、自分の子どもから目を離さないようにしないとなりません。目を離すといなくなってしまいます。

▶▶ "an eye" は抽象的な「見ること、注意」といった意味を指している。

Let's Review

10 My girlfriend is very _____ English Idioms.

僕のガールフレンドは、英語のイディオムにすっかり夢中だ。

11 She had to _____ Bill Gates to fix the computer.

彼女はビル・ゲイツにコンピュータを修理するようしつこく言わねばならなかった。

12 You always have to _____ your children at all times, when you look away they disappear.

いつでも必ず、自分の子どもから目を離さないようにしないとなりません。目を離すといなくなってしまいます。

解答 **10** keen on learn about **11** keep after **12** keep an eye on

DAY 25

01 keep one's nose clean
動 句 スラング 品行方正である

When you keep your nose clean, you don't have to worry about the rumors.
品行方正にしていれば、噂を心配する必要はありません。

▶▶ stay out of trouble と同義。

---

02 keep the ball rolling
動 句 インフォーマル 途切れないようにうまく続けていく

You have to build up momentum to keep the ball rolling.
途切れないようにうまく続けていくには、勢いを強くしなければなりません。

▶▶ start the ball rolling は「何かを始める」という意味。

---

03 keep up with the Joneses
動 句 人に負けまいと見栄をはる

Stop trying to keep up with the Joneses. Make your own imprint and name known.
人に負けまいと見栄をはろうとするのをやめましょう。自身の印象を残し、名前が知られるようにしましょう。

▶▶ 米国の漫画家 Arthur R. Momand が 1913 年から 28 年間新聞に連載した『Keeping Up with the Joneses』というマンガから。

Let's Review

01 When you _____, you don't have to worry about the rumors.

品行方正にしていれば、噂を心配する必要はありません。

02 You have to build up momentum to _____.

途切れないようにうまく続けていくには、勢いを強くしなければなりません。

03 Stop trying to _____.
Make your own imprint and name known.

人に負けまいと見栄をはろうとするのをやめましょう。自身の印象を残し、名前が知られるようにしましょう。

解答 **01** keep your nose clean **02** keep the ball rolling **03** keep up with the Joneses

DAY 25

04 keyed up
形 インフォーマル 緊張した

Jobs is keyed up about his presentation next week.
ジョブズは来週のプレゼンテーションのことで緊張している。

▶▶ keyed up to the roof になると「酔っぱらう」という意味。

---

05 kick the bucket
動 句 スラング 死ぬ

The patient finally kicked the bucket this year.
その患者はついに今年亡くなった。

▶▶ 首つり自殺をするときに、バケツの上に乗って首をロープにかけてからバケツを蹴っ飛ばすことから。

---

06 kick up one's heels
動 句 インフォーマル はしゃぎ回る

Eva went to a club and kicked up her heels.
エヴァはクラブに行ってはしゃぎ回った。

▶▶ 楽しそうに後脚ではねている馬の様子から。

Let's Review

04 Jobs is _____ about his presentation next week.

ジョブズは来週のプレゼンテーションのことで緊張している。

05 The patient finally _____ this year.

その患者はついに今年亡くなった。

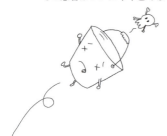

06 Eva went to a club and _____.

エヴァはクラブに行ってはしゃぎ回った。

解答 **04** keyed up　**05** kicked the bucket　**06** kicked up her heels

DAY 25

07 kill time
動 句 時間をつぶす

She is killing time in Starbucks before heading to the train station.

彼女は電車の駅に向かう前に、スターバックスで時間をつぶしている。

▶▶ kill には「(時間を)つぶす」という意味がある。

---

08 knock about
動 ぶらつく、放浪する

Mark spent a few months knocking about New York City.

マークは数か月間、ニューヨーク市を放浪して過ごした。

▶▶ about には「(漠然と)〜の周辺に」という意味がある。

---

09 knock oneself out
動 句 インフォーマル 全力を出す

Brian and David knocked themselves out running a business.

ブライアンとデイヴィッドは、全力でビジネスの運営に当たった。

▶▶ 相手の希望に対して「勝手にやれば?」と無関心に肯定する返答は "Knock yourself out."

Let's Review

07 She is _____ in Starbucks before heading to the train station.

彼女は電車の駅に向かう前に、スターバックスで時間をつぶしている。

08 Mark spent a few months _____ New York City.

マークは数か月間、ニューヨーク市を放浪して過ごした。

09 Brian and David _____ running a business.

ブライアンとデイヴィッドは、全力でビジネスの運営に当たった。

解答 **07** killing time   **08** knocking about   **09** knocked themselves out

DAY 25

know where one stands
動 句 (人が)自分のことをどう思っているか知っている

I would really like to know where I stand.

私は、人にどう思われているかを本当に知りたいの。

▶▶ know which end it up と同義。

---

landslide
名 圧倒的勝利

If Obama gets this budget package done, he wins re-election in a landslide.

オバマがこの予算法案を可決すれば、再選挙で圧倒的な勝利を収めるだろう。

▶▶「辛勝」は narrow vicory。

---

last but not least
副 句 最後になるが決して重要度は低くない

And now, last but not least, I will give the present to Steve, who will make the presentation.

さあそして、最後に忘れてはならないこととして、プレゼンテーションを行うスティーブに贈り物を渡します。

▶▶ しばしば、人を紹介するときなどに使われる。

Let's Review

10 I would really like to _____.

私は、人にどう思われているかを本当に知りたいの。

11 If Obama gets this budget package done, he wins re-election in a _____.

オバマがこの予算法案を可決すれば、再選挙で圧倒的な勝利を収めるだろう。

12 And now, _____, I will give the present to Steve, who will make the presentation.

さあそして、最後に忘れてはならないこととして、プレゼンテーションを行うスティーブに贈り物を渡します。

解答 **10** know where I stand **11** landslide **12** last but not least

DAY 26

01 laundry list
名 句 長いリスト

I got a laundry list to do this weekend.
今週行うべきことの長いリストを受け取った。

▶▶ 海外のホテルには、多くの洗濯アイテムをリストした Laundry list が置いてある。ここから長々とした一覧表を指す言葉になった。

02 lay a finger on
動 句 〜を的確に指摘する、〜に指を触れる

Don't you dare lay a finger on my MacBook.
僕の MacBook に手を触れるなんてことはするな。

Only I can fight with my sister, if you lay a finger on her, you die!
妹とけんかしていいのは僕だけだ、あいつに指1本触れてみろ、死ぬぞ!

▶▶ 少しでも触ったら…、というニュアンス。通常否定文で使う。

03 lay away
動 ❶貯蓄する

Warren laid a little of his pay away each month.
ウォーレンは毎月、給料のうち少額を貯蓄していた。

❷葬る
The soldier was laid away in the National Cemetery.
その兵士は、国立墓地に葬られた。

▶▶「商品を取り置きしてもらう」という意味もある。

Let's Review

01 I got a _____ to do this weekend.

今週行うべきことの長いリストを受け取った。

02 Only I can fight with my sister, if you _____ her, you die!

妹とけんかしていいのは僕だけだ、あいつに指1本触れてみろ、死ぬぞ！

03 Warren _____ a little of his pay _____ each month.

ウォーレンは毎月、給料のうち少額を貯蓄していた。

解答 **01** laundry list **02** lay a finger on **03** laid away

DAY 26

04 lead off
動 ～を始める、口火を切る

Choo led off the All-Star Major League Baseball game with a home run.
メジャーリーグのオールスターゲームはチョーのホームランで始まった。

▶▶ lead-off man は野球のトップバッターのこと。

---

05 lean on
動 句 スラング ～に圧力をかける

She has been leaning on Mark not to smoke.
彼女はマークに、タバコを吸わないように圧力をかけ続けていた。

▶▶ lean on には「(～に)寄りかかる、もたれる」という意味もある。

---

06 leave no stone unturned
動 句 あらゆる手立てをつくす

Ophelia left no stone unturned to get married to David.
オフィーリアはデイヴィッドと結婚するためにあらゆる手立てをつくした。

▶▶ 同様の表現に move heaven and earth「全力をつくす」がある。

Let's Review

04 Choo _____ the All-Star Major League Baseball game with a home run.

メジャーリーグのオールスターゲームはチョーのホームランで始まった。

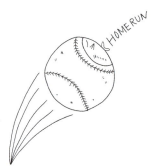

05 She has been _____ Mark not to smoke.

彼女はマークに、タバコを吸わないように圧力をかけ続けていた。

06 Ophelia _____ to get married to David.

オフィーリアはデイヴィッドと結婚するためにあらゆる手立てをつくした。

解答 **04** led off　**05** leaning on　**06** left no stone unturned

DAY 26

07 let down
動句 失望させる、がっかりさせる

Next time, I am not gonna let you down.
次はあなたを失望させません。

▶▶ let up は「(雨・痛み・非難などが) 弱まる、くつろぐ、〜する手をゆるめる」という意味。

08 let bygones be bygones
動句 過去のことは水に流す

Let's just let bygones be bygones. I think we can start over fresh, and be all good.
さあ、これまでのことは水に流そう。僕たちはもう一度やり直せると思うんだ、そしてすべてうまくいくよ。

▶▶ bygones は「過ぎ去ったこと、過去のこと」。

09 let go of
動句 〜を手放す

As soon as she let go of the leash, the dog ran away.
彼女がリードから手を離すとすぐ、その犬は走って逃げだした。

▶▶ let 〜 go は「〜を (拘束している状態から) 解放する」という意味。

Let's Review

07 Next time, I am not gonna _____.

次はあなたを失望させません。

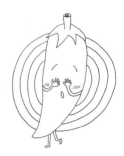

08 Let's just _____.

I think we can start over fresh, and be all good.

さあ、これまでのことは水に流そう。僕たちはもう一度やり直せると思うんだ、そしてすべてうまくいくよ。

09 As soon as she _____ the leash, the dog ran away.

彼女がリードから手を離すとすぐ、その犬は走って逃げだした。

解答 **07** let you down **08** let bygones be bygones **09** let go of

⑩ let one's hair down
動 句 インフォーマル くつろぐ、羽を伸ばす

Zuckerberg graduates tomorrow and time to let his hair down on Saturday with his friends.
ザッカーバーグは明日卒業し、土曜日は友人と羽を伸ばすときだ。

▶▶ 昔、女性が人前では髪を結い上げていて、それをほどくのは家族や親しい人の前でくつろいでいるときに限られていたことから。

⑪ let the cat out of the bag
動 句 インフォーマル 秘密を漏らす

Do we let the cat out of the bag or leave it as an eternal enigma?
秘密を漏らしますか、または永遠の謎のままにしておきますか？

▶▶ 昔、英国では子豚を袋に入れて取引していたが、悪徳商人が偽って猫を代わりに入れて売っていたという。袋を開けるとウソがバレることから。

⑫ level playing field
名 句 平等（公平）な条件

Anyone who thinks this game is a level playing field is an idiot.
この試合が公平な条件で行なわれたと考える人がいたら大馬鹿ものだ。

▶▶ level は「平坦な」という意味。

Let's Review

10 Zuckerberg graduates tomorrow and time to _____ on Saturday with his friends.

ザッカーバーグは明日卒業し、土曜日は友人と羽を伸ばすときだ。

11 Do we _____ or leave it as an eternal enigma?

秘密を漏らしますか、または永遠の謎のままにしておきますか？

12 Anyone who thinks this game is a _____ is an idiot.

この試合が平等な条件で行なわれたと考える人がいたら大馬鹿ものだ。

解答 **10** let his hair down **11** let the cat out of the bag **12** level playing field

DAY 27

01 life and limb
名 生命と身体

Julia risked life and limb to save her child.
ジュリアは自分の子どもを助けるために生命を危険にさらした。

▶▶ risk life and limb で「生命の危険を冒す」。stick one's neck out と同義。

---

02 light up
動 明るくなる

Brian's face lit up when he saw the unopened Pringles.
未開封のプリングルを見たとき、ブライアンの顔は明るくなった。

▶▶ 街中の建物や樹木などを照明で照らすという意味の「ライトアップ」は和製英語。

---

03 like two peas in a pod
形 句 うり二つ

Julia and her son are like two peas in a pod.
ジュリアと息子はうり二つだ。

▶▶ as like as (two) eggs と同義。

Let's Review

01 Julia risked _____ to save her child.

ジュリアは自分の子どもを助けるために生命を危険にさらした。

02 Brian's face _____ when he saw the unopened Pringles.

未開封のプリングルを見たとき、ブライアンの顔は明るくなった。

03 Julia and her son are _____.

ジュリアと息子はうり二つだ。

解答 **01** life and limb **02** lit up **03** like two peas in a pod

DAY 27

live from hand to mouth
動 句 その日暮らしをする

David was earning five dollars an hour working at the store. He was living from hand to mouth.

デイヴィッドはその店で働き、1時間に5ドル稼いでいた。彼はその日暮らしの生活を送っていた。

▶▶ 手に入ったものをすぐ口にもっていくことから。

---

live it up
動 句 インフォーマル 楽しい時間を過ごす

I have a lot of childhood memories. I think I lived it up.

僕には子どもの頃の思い出がたくさんある。楽しい時間を過ごしたと思う。

▶▶ liven up で「活気づける、景気をつける」。

---

living end
形 スラング 最高

Wu-Tang Clan's concert we saw last night was the living end.

私たちが昨夜観たウータン・クランのコンサートは最高だった。

▶▶ end には「最高のもの」という意味がある (米俗)。

Let's Review

04 David was earning five dollars an hour working at the store. He was _____.

デイヴィッドはその店で働き、1時間に5ドル稼いでいた。彼はその日暮らしの生活を送っていた。

05 I have a lot of childhood memories. I think I _____.

僕には子どもの頃の思い出がたくさんある。楽しい時間を過ごしたと思う。

06 Wu-Tang Clan's concert we saw last night was the _____.

私たちが昨夜観たウータン・クランのコンサートは最高だった。

解答　**04** living from hand to mouth　**05** lived it up　**06** living end

07 look out
動 〜に用心する

I am planning to head from NY to visit friends near Florida. Any roads I should look out for?

ニューヨークを出発して、フロリダ近くの友人を訪ねようと計画しているんだ。用心すべき道はあるかなあ？

▶▶ Be careful. よりも強い注意を促す。

---

08 lose one's heart
動 句 心を奪われる

I have lost my heart to someone who can't be mine.

私は自分のものとはなりえないものに心を奪われている。

▶▶ fall in love と同義。

---

09 lose touch
動 句 インフォーマル 〜との連絡が途絶えている

I have lost touch with everyone except 3 people.

私は3人以外すべての人との連絡が途絶えている。

▶▶ 反意語は in touch with。

Let's Review

07 I am planning to head from NY to visit friends near Florida. Any roads I should _____ for?

ニューヨークを出発して、フロリダ近くの友人を訪ねようと計画しているんだ。用心すべき道はあるかなあ？

08 I have _____ to someone who can't be mine.

私は自分のものとはなりえないものに心を奪われている。

09 I have _____ with everyone except 3 people.

私は3人以外すべての人との連絡が途絶えている。

解答　**07** look out　**08** lost my heart　**09** lost touch

DAY 27

10 big mouth
名 スラング おしゃべり

If you didn't see it with your own eyes, don't share it with your big mouth.

自分自身の目でそれを見ていないのならば、ぺらぺらとしゃべるな。

▶▶ 日本語でいう"ビッグマウス"(大口をたたく人)ではなく、「おしゃべりで口が軽い人」という意味。

---

11 mad about
形 句 ❶ かんかんに怒る

What is Eva so mad about?　エヴァは何をそんなに怒っているの？

❷ ～が大好きだ

Julia's always been mad about kids.

ジュリアはいつだってずっと子どもが大好きだった。

▶▶ 語源は mad の本来の意味「気が狂った」から。

---

12 main squeeze
名 スラング ❶ トップ、ボス、重要人物

Marlon Brando is the main squeeze of this organization.

マーロン・ブランドが、この組織のトップだ。

❷ 恋人

Emma Stone's main squeeze is Andrew Garfield.

エマ・ストーンの恋人は、アンドリュー・ガーフィールドだ。

▶▶ 「重要人物」の方の語源は不明だが、「恋人」は squeeze の意味のひとつである「抱きしめる」から。

Let's Review

10 If you didn't see it with your own eyes, don't share it with your _____.

自分自身の目でそれを見ていないのならば、べらべらとしゃべるな。

11 What is Eva so _____?

エヴァは何をそんなに怒っているの？

12 Emma Stone's _____ is Andrew Garfield.

エマ・ストーンの恋人は、アンドリュー・ガーフィールドだ。

解答 **10** big mouth **11** mad about **12** main squeeze

DAY 28

01 make a mountain out of a molehill
動 句 ささいなことを大げさに言う

Don't make a mountain out of a molehill. Just step over it.

ささいなことを大げさに言うな。それを乗り越えて行け。

▶▶ 類似表現に lay it on thick, blow ～ all out of proportion。

02 make-believe
名 見せかけ、架空のもの

The creatures of Godzilla are all make-believe.

ゴジラという生物は、まったく架空のものだ。

▶▶ 動詞形の make believe「～のふりをする、～のように見せ掛ける」は make people believe that「～を人に信じさせる」の people が省略されたもの。

03 make ends meet
動 句 収支内でやりくりする

The younger generation in the world today is working hard just to make ends meet.

今日の世界において、若年世代は、収支内でやりくりするだけのために必死に働いている。

▶▶ make both ends meet とも言う。句動詞だと balance out。

Let's Review

01 Don't _____
_____.
Just step over it.

ささいなことを大げさに言うな。それを乗り越えて行け。

02 The creatures of Godzilla are all _____.

ゴジラという生物は、まったく架空のものだ。

03 The younger generation in the world today is working hard just to _____.

今日の世界において、若年世代は、収支内でやりくりするだけのために必死に働いている。

解答 **01** make a mountain out of a molehill **02** make-believe **03** make ends meet

DAY 28

04 make eyes at
動 句　インフォーマル　色目を使う

There's no excuse for my girl to make eyes at anyone other than me.

恋人が僕以外の誰かに色目を使うのは、どんな理由があっても許されない。

▶▶ 同様の表現に cast amorous glances at, give someone the eye, roll one's eyes at。

05 make hay while the sun shines
動 句　好機を逃さない

It is perfect weather for scoring and the players must make hay while the sun shines.

得点するには申し分のない天候だから、プレイヤーは好機を逃さないようにしないとならない。

▶▶ 諺より。類句に Time and tide wait for no man.「歳月人を待たず」、He who hesitates is lost.「ためらう者は敗れる」、Opportunity seldom knocks twice.「好機が二度訪れることはほとんどない」。

06 make neither head nor tail of
動 句　理解できない

English Idioms are so confused that I can make neither head nor tail of it without this book.

英語のイディオムはとても複雑なので、この本なしでは理解できない。

▶▶ head and tail にはコインの表と裏という意味もある。

Let's Review

04 There's no excuse for my girl to _____ anyone other than me.

恋人が僕以外の誰かに色目を使うのは、どんな理由があっても許されない。

05 It is perfect weather for scoring and the players must _____ _____.

得点するには申し分のない天候だから、プレイヤーは好機を逃さないようにしないとならない。

06 English Idioms are so confused that I can _____ it without this book.

英語のイディオムはとても複雑なので、この本なしでは理解できない。

解答 **04** make eyes at　**05** make hay while the sun shines　**06** make neither head nor tail of

DAY 28

07 make one's head spin
動句 くらくらする

Marketing meetings make my head spin, but in a great way!
マーケティング会議で頭がくらくらしたが、それは素晴らしいほうにだ！

▶▶ make someone's head go around, make someone dizzy と同義。

08 make one's mark
動句 成功する

Some Tattoo artists hope to make their mark in Florida.
タトゥーのアーティストの中には、フロリダで成功したいと思っている人もいる。

▶▶ make a name for oneself と同義。

09 make one's mouth water
動句 よだれを流させる

New Burger King Whopper made her mouth water.
新しいバーガーキングのワッパーは、彼女によだれを流させた。

▶▶ mouth-watering は「よだれの出そうな、おいしそうな」。

Let's Review

 Marketing meetings _____, but in a great way!

マーケティング会議で頭がくらくらしたが、それは素晴らしいほうにだ！

 Some Tattoo artists hope to _____ in Florida.

タトゥーのアーティストの中には、フロリダで成功したいと思っている人もいる。

New Burger King Whopper _____.

新しいバーガーキングのワッパーは、彼女によだれを流させた。

解答 07 make my head spin 08 make their mark 09 made her mouth water

⑩ make up one's mind
動句 決心する

I seriously wish Julia would make her mind very soon.
ジュリアがすぐに心を決めるよう、私は本気で望んでいる。

▶▶ give up in one's mind「内心あきらめる、気持ちの整理がつく」、pop up in one's mind「心にパッと思い浮かぶ」

⑪ man in the street
名句 一般の人々

The man in the street has little interest in history.
一般人は歴史にほとんど興味がない。

▶▶ ニュースメディアで、事件などの目撃情報や選挙の予想を一般市民から聞くときなどに使われる。

⑫ matter of course
名句 当然のこと

Brian resets browsers and clear cookies every few days as a matter of course.
ブライアンは当然のこととして数日おきにブラウザをリセットし、クッキーを消去する。

▶▶ foregone conclusion と同義。

Let's Review

10 I seriously wish Julia would _____ very soon.

ジュリアがすぐに心を決めるよう、私は本気で望んでいる。

11 The _____ has little interest in history.

一般人は歴史にほとんど興味がない。

12 Brian resets browsers and clear cookies every few days as a _____.

ブライアンは当然のこととして数日おきにブラウザをリセットし、クッキーを消去する。

解答 **10** make up her mind **11** man in the street **12** matter of course

DAY 29

01 meet up with
動句 (人)に会う、(人)と集まる

Mark met up with some very wise people while in New York City. They have made Mark realize that he hold a powerful deck of cards.

マークはニューヨーク市にいる間に、非常に頭のいい人々と会った。彼らのおかげでマークは、自分が強力なカードの一組を手にしていることを実感した。

▶▶ オンラインで知り合った人と初めて会うときにも使われる。

02 mend one's ways
動句 行いを改める、改心する

I am trying to mend my ways. Acceptance is the first step to change.

私は行いを改めようとしている。受け入れることが変化への第一歩だ。

▶▶ 昔は mend one's manners と言っていた。

03 mess around
動句 うろうろする、ふざけ回る

Time to stop messing around and talk about the important stuff.

ふざけるのはやめて、重要なことを話すべき時だ。

▶▶ 「ぶらぶらして過ごす」の他の表現: fart around, fool around, muck around/about

Let's Review

01 Mark _____ some very wise people while in New York City. They have made Mark realize that he hold a powerful deck of cards.

マークはニューヨーク市にいる間に、非常に頭のいい人々と会った。彼らのおかげでマークは、自分が強力なカードの一組を手にしていることを実感した。

02 I am trying to _____. Acceptance is the first step to change.

私は行いを改めようとしている。受け入れることが変化への第一歩だ。

03 Time to stop _____ and talk about the important stuff.

ふざけるのはやめて、重要なことを話すべき時だ。

解答 **01** met up with　**02** mend my ways　**03** messing around

DAY 29

04 monkey on one's back
名 句 (不愉快な人に)(取り除くのが困難な)厄介な問題、重荷

Julia's boss is a real monkey on her back.
ジュリアの上司は実にやっかいだ。

▶▶ monkey on the house は「家のローン」。

---

05 more the merrier
名 句 人が多ければ多いほど楽しい

"Can I bring Eva to a party?" "Sure, the more the merrier!"
「エヴァをパーティーに連れてきていい？」「いいとも、たくさんの人が来た方が楽しいよ！」

▶▶ The more the merrier; the fewer the better fare.「人数が多いほど楽しく、人数の少ない方がたくさん食べられる」《諺》

---

06 morning after
名 スラング 二日酔い、苦しい目覚め

Mark woke up with a big headache and knew it was the morning after.
マークはひどい頭痛で目が覚めて、二日酔いだと気づいた。

▶▶ hangover と同義。

Let's Review

04 Julia's boss is a real
_____.

ジュリアの上司は実にやっかいだ。

05 "Can I bring Eva to a party?" "Sure, the _____!"

「エヴァをパーティーに連れてきていい？」「いいとも、たくさんの人が来た方が楽しいよ！」

06 Mark woke up with a big headache and knew it was the _____.

マークはひどい頭痛で目が覚めて、二日酔いだと気づいた。

解答　**04** monkey on her back　**05** more the merrier　**06** morning after

DAY 29

move heaven and earth
動 句 あらゆる手をつくす

When you really love someone, you would move heaven and earth just to be with her.

本当に誰かを愛したら、その人と一緒にいるためだけのために、君は何でもするだろう。

▶▶ 同様の表現に leave no stone unturned「調べつくす、あらゆる手段をつくす」。

mum is the word
秘密にする

Mark and Eva are planning a surprise birthday party for Julia and mum is the word.

マークとエヴァはジュリアのためにサプライズ・パーティーを計画中であり、このことは秘密にしている。

▶▶ Mum は、口を閉じて発する音。シェークスピアの作品『ヘンリー4世 (Henry IV)』に出てくるセリフ "Seal your lips and give no words but mum." より。

music to one's ears
名 句 耳に心地よく響くもの、聞いて嬉しいこと

Beautiful lady on the phone was speaking French. It's like music to my ears.

電話の向こうの美しい女性はフランス語を話していた。それは私の耳に心地よく響いた。

▶▶ music を使った他の表現：face the music「(自分の行為の結果に対して)進んで責任を取る、潔く結果を受け止める」

Let's Review

07 When you really love someone, you would _____ just to be with her.

本当に誰かを愛したら、その人と一緒にいるためだけのために、君は何でもするだろう。

08 Mark and Eva are planning a surprise birthday party for Julia and _____.

マークとエヴァはジュリアのためにサプライズ・パーティーを計画中であり、このことは秘密にしている。

09 Beautiful lady on the phone was speaking French. It's like _____.

電話の向こうの美しい女性はフランス語を話していた。それは私の耳に心地よく響いた。

解答　**07** move heaven and earth　**08** mum is the word　**09** music to my ears

DAY 29

⑩ my lips are sealed
インフォーマル 秘密を守る

You can tell me what happened. My lips are sealed.

何があったか僕に話していいんだ。秘密は守るよ。

▶▶ 同様の表現に "Your secret is safe with me."

---

⑪ nail down
動句 インフォーマル 確定させる、(約束などに)縛りつける

We need to get these plans nailed down.

私たちはこれらの計画を確定させる必要がある。

▶▶ nail down to は「〈人を〉(～に)同意させる；〈人に〉はっきり言わせる」。

---

⑫ namedropper
名 ネームドロッパー、有名人の名前を知人であるかのように使って、自慢をする人

Since he met Jay-Z on the street by chance he has become a namedropper.

彼は道で偶然ジェイ-Z に出会ってから、知り合いのようにふるまうようになった。

▶▶ その他の dropper: dime dropper「密告者」、jaw-dropper「あっと驚くもの」eye dropper「目薬容器」。

Let's Review

10 You can tell me what happened.

_____.

何があったか僕に話していいんだ。秘密は守るよ。

11 We need to get these plans _____.

私たちはこれらの計画を確定させる必要がある。

12 Since he met Jay-Z on the street by chance he has become a _____.

彼は道で偶然ジェイ-Z に出会ってから、知り合いのようにふるまうようになった。

解答 **10** My lips are sealed　**11** nailed down　**12** namedropper

DAY 30

01 no doubt
副 疑いもなく、たぶん

Someday the sea levels will rise. No doubt that Japan will be among the most severely affected.

いつの日か、海面は上昇するだろう。日本は、もっとも深刻な影響を受けるうちの一つになることは疑いない。

▶▶ 他に without/beyond doubt。

02 no sweat
形 スラング 簡単な、たやすい

Job transferring was no sweat for Mark.

マークにとって、仕事を変わるのはたやすかった。

▶▶ sweat には「つらい［骨の折れる・つまらない］仕事」という意味がある。

03 nutty as a fruitcake
形 句 頭のおかしい

How come every woman named Elena is as nutty as a fruitcake?

エレナという名前の女は、どうしてみんな頭がおかしいんだ？

▶▶ 同義語に barmy, daffy, dotty, loopy, wacky, zany など。

Let's Review

01 Someday the sea levels will rise. _____ that Japan will be among the most severely affected.

いつの日か、海面は上昇するだろう。日本は、もっとも深刻な影響を受けるうちの一つになることは疑いない。

02 Job transferring was _____ for Mark.

マークにとって、仕事を変わるのはたやすかった。

03 How come every woman named Elena is as _____?

エレナという名前の女は、どうしてみんな頭がおかしいんだ？

解答　**01** No doubt　**02** no sweat　**03** nutty as a fruitcake

DAY 30

04 oddball
名 スラング インフォーマル 風変わりな(人)

Eva is an oddball. Hands down.

エヴァは変人だ。間違いない。

▶▶ 類似表現に odd stick「変わり者」、odd fish「変人」

---

05 off the hook
副 句 苦境から救う

Superman got Spider-man off the hook, but they didn't have the antidote to the ailment.

スーパーマンはスパイダーマンを苦境から救ったが、彼らは病気の解毒剤を持っていなかった。

▶▶ しばしば動詞 get, let を伴う。

---

06 off the record
副 句 非公式に、オフレコで

"Off the record," the boss said, "you will get a good raise for next year, but you'll have to wait for your official letter."

「非公式だが」と上司が言った。「来年は十分な昇給が得られるが、正式な通知を待たなくてはならないだろう。」

▶▶ go on record は「公言する、公表する」。

Let's Review

04 Eva is an _____.
Hands down.

エヴァは変人だ。間違いない。

05 Superman got Spider-man _____, but they didn't have the antidote to the ailment.

スーパーマンはスパイダーマンを苦境から救ったが、彼らは病気の解毒剤を持っていなかった。

06 "_____," the boss said, "you will get a good raise for next year, but you'll have to wait for your official letter."

「非公式だが」と上司が言った。「来年は十分な昇給が得られるが、正式な通知を待たなくてはならないだろう。」

解答 **04** oddball **05** off the hook **06** Off the record

DAY 30

 off the top of one's head
副句 インフォーマル すぐに思いついて

I need some more good friends in my life. I can probably only name two off the top of my head.

私の人生にはもっと良い友達が数人必要だ。すぐに名前を思いつけるのは、おそらく2人だけだ。

▶▶「すぐ思い出せるのは、直感的には」、または「確かね、多分ね」というニュアンス。

 once and for all
副句 これきりで（止める）

Let me tell you some tips to help you quit smoking once and for all.

これきりで煙草を止める手助けになる秘訣をいくつか教えましょう。

▶▶ one last time「最後にもう一度（だけ）」は、とりあえず今回はここまでにしておこう、というニュアンス。

 once in a blue moon
副句 ごくまれに

Julia loves her natural hair but once in a blue moon she likes to get crazy with it. She currently has blue hair.

ジュリアは自然な髪が好きだが、ごくまれにおかしなことをしたがる。いまは青い髪をしているよ。

▶▶ 空中の微細なチリで時折だが月が青く見えることがあることから。

Let's Review

07 I need some more good friends in my life. I can probably only name two _____.

私の人生にはもっと良い友達が数人必要だ。すぐに名前を思いつけるのは、おそらく2人だけだ。

08 Let me tell you some tips to help you quit smoking _____.

これきりで煙草を止める手助けになる秘訣をいくつか教えましょう。

09 Julia loves her natural hair but _____ she likes to get crazy with it. She currently has blue hair.

ジュリアは自然な髪が好きだが、ごくまれにおかしなことをしたがる。いまは青い髪をしているよ。

解答 **07** off the top of my head **08** once and for all **09** once in a blue moon

on cloud nine
形句 スラング 有頂天になって

After memorizing all the English Idioms in this book, Mark was on cloud nine with his foreign friends.

この本の英語のイディオムをすべて覚えた後、マークは外国の友人たちと一緒に有頂天になっていた。

▶▶ 語源は、ダンテの『神曲』から、または米国の気象庁で用いられている雲の9区分からなど、諸説ありはっきりしない。

on easy street
形句 インフォーマル 裕福な身分

My friend grew up on easy street.

僕の友人は裕福に育った。

▶▶ easy street は「裕福な［金持ちの］身分」のこと。

one on the city
名 スラング （飲食店で出される）1杯の水

Julia asked the Outback crew for one on the city.

ジュリアはアウトバックのスタッフに1杯の水を頼んだ。

▶▶ ダイナー（軽食レストラン）やレストランの隠語のひとつ。同義語に eighty-one。なお、Outback はステーキレストランチェーンのひとつ。crew は「店員」の意味。

Let's Review

10 After memorizing all the English Idioms in this book, Mark was _____ with his foreign friends.

この本の英語のイディオムをすべて覚えた後、マークは外国の友人たちと一緒に有頂天になっていた。

11 My friend grew up _____.

僕の友人は裕福に育った。

12 Julia asked the Outback crew for _____.

ジュリアはアウトバックのスタッフに１杯の水を頼んだ。

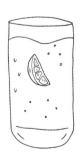

解答 **10** on cloud nine **11** on easy street **12** one on the city

DAY 31

01 on one's knees
形 句 ひざまずく、ひざまずいて嘆願する

If you open the window, you'll see me on my knees for the concert ticket.

窓を開ければ、コンサートのチケット欲しさに僕がひざまずいているのが見えるよ。

▶▶ on one's hands and knees だと「四つん這いになって」。

02 on purpose
副 句 故意に

I don't get why some people would spell things wrong on purpose. Don't you feel ashamed spelling 'Agen' instead of 'again'?

私はわざとスペルを間違える人たちが理解できない。「again」を「Agen」と書いて恥ずかしくないのかな？

▶▶ intentionally, deliberately と同義。

03 on the dot
副 句 インフォーマル 時間通りに、即座に

Every morning at 08:00 a.m. on the dot, my wife wakes me up, every single day.

毎朝8時きっかりに妻は僕を起こす。毎日だ。

▶▶ 時計の文字盤上の時間を刻む点に、時計の針がちょうど重なっている様子。

Let's Review

01 If you open the window, you'll see me _____ for the concert ticket.

窓を開ければ、コンサートのチケット欲しさに僕がひざまずいているのが見えるよ。

02 I don't get why some people would spell things wrong _____. Don't you feel ashamed spelling 'Agen' instead of 'again'?

私はわざとスペルを間違える人たちが理解できない。「again」を「Agen」と書いて恥ずかしくないのかな？

03 Every morning at 08:00 a.m. _____, my wife wakes me up, every single day.

毎朝8時きっかりに妻は僕を起こす。毎日だ。

解答 **01** on my knees **02** on purpose **03** on the dot

DAY 31

04 on the double
副句 ただちに、大急ぎで

I need something to eat. On the double please.

私には食べる物が必要だ。大急ぎで頼みます。

▶▶ 元は軍隊用語で「2倍の速さで行進せよ」→「急げ！」という意味。

---

05 on the homestretch
副句 最終段階に入って

"You haven't finished yet?" "I am on the homestretch."

「君はまだ終わっていないの？」「僕は最終段階だよ」

▶▶ homestretch は競争や競馬などにおいてのゴール前の最終直線コースのこと。

---

06 on the house
形句 インフォーマル 経営者のおごりで、無料で

At the launching symposium, the food was on the house.

その発表シンポジウムでは、食べ物が無料だった。

▶▶ ホテルやレストラン、バーなどでの食べ物や飲み物についての表現。

Let's Review

04 I need something to eat. _____ please.

私には食べる物が必要だ。大急ぎで頼みます。

05 "You haven't finished yet?" "I am _____."

「君はまだ終わっていないの？」「僕は最終段階だよ」

06 At the launching symposium, the food was _____.

その発表シンポジウムでは、食べ物が無料だった。

解答 **04** On the double **05** on the homestretch **06** on the house

DAY 31

 on the market
形 句 売りに出ている、市場に出回っている

Many kinds of Samsung laptop are on the market.
さまざまな種類のサムスンのラップトップが市場に出回っている。

▶▶ I'm on the market. は「恋人募集中」。

---

 on the same page with
副 句 同じ考えを持っている

Mark is on the same page with Brian since they decided to go on a business together.
2人が事業を一緒に続けると決めてから、マークはブライアンと同じ考えを持っている。

▶▶ 「あたかもお互いに同じ本の同じページを読んでいるかのように」という意味。

---

 on the tip of one's tongue
副 句 喉まで出かかって

I've got a top secret and it's on the tip of my tongue.
私はトップシークレットを知っており、それが喉まで出かかっている。

▶▶ 日本語だと「のど元」だが、英語では「舌の先」。

Let's Review

07 Many kinds of Samsung laptop are _____.

さまざまな種類のサムスンのラップトップが市場に出回っている。

08 Mark is _____ Brian since they decided to go on a business together.

２人が事業を一緒に続けると決めてから、マークはブライアンと同じ考えを持っている。

09 I've got a top secret and it's _____.

私はトップシークレットを知っており、それが喉まで出かかっている。

解答 **07** on the market　**08** on the same page with　**09** on the tip of my tongue

DAY 31

out of place
形 句 不適当な、場違いの

Do you ever feel out of place? Like somehow you just don't belong and no one understands you.

あなたはこれまでに、場違いだと感じたことはありますか？ 何となく居心地が悪くて、誰もあなたを理解していないような心持ちです。

▶▶ out of には「～の範囲外に、～を超越して」などの意味もある。

out of this world
形 句 スラング 飛びきり素晴らしい

The designer's new iPad cases are out of this world!

そのデザイナーの新しい iPad ケースは、飛びきり素晴らしい！

▶▶「(この世のものとは思えないくらい) とても素晴らしい」という意味。

out of whack
形 句 スラング 具合が悪い、(～と)一致しない

I think I'm going to go to a chiropractor. My neck is definitely out of whack.

カイロプラクティックに行こうと思う。間違いなく首の具合が悪いんだ。

▶▶ in fine whack は「とても調子がいい」。

Let's Review

10 Do you ever feel _____?
Like somehow you just don't belong and no one understands you.

あなたはこれまでに、場違いだと感じたことはありますか？ 何となく居心地が悪くて、誰もあなたを理解していないような心持ちです。

11 The designer's new iPad cases are _____!

そのデザイナーの新しい iPad ケースは、飛びきり素晴らしい！

12 I think I'm going to go to a chiropractor. My neck is definitely _____.

カイロプラクティックに行こうと思う。間違いなく首の具合が悪いんだ。

解答 **10** out of place **11** out of this world **12** out of whack

01 pain in the ass
名 スラング イライラさせる、うんざりさせる、悩みの種

I love my long mermaid hair, but it is a pain in the ass to take care of it.
自分の長いマーメイドヘアは大好きだけれど、手入れをするのにうんざりさせられる。

▶▶ ass 以外にも (pain in the) ankle/balls/butt/neck/rear/rump など多くの表現がある。

02 palm off
動 インフォーマル だまして〜を押し付ける

Why is he always trying to palm off counterfeit watches to me?
どうして彼はいつも私に偽物の時計をつかませようとするのだろう？

▶▶ その物を相手に渡すまで、手のひらで隠して見せないでおく様子を表す。

03 pass away
動 亡くなる

My grandma passed away like a year ago but I still miss her.
祖母は一年ほど前に亡くなったが、私はいまでも祖母が恋しい。

▶▶ die のやや婉曲的な表現。pass on/over とも言う。

Let's Review

01 I love my long mermaid hair, but it is a _____ to take care of it.

自分の長いマーメイドヘアは大好きだけれど、手入れをするのにうんざりさせられる。

02 Why is he always trying to _____ counterfeit watches to me?

どうして彼はいつも私に偽物の時計をつかませようとするのだろう？

03 My grandma _____ like a year ago but I still miss her.

祖母は一年ほど前に亡くなったが、私はいまでも祖母が恋しい。

解答　**01** pain in the ass　**02** palm off　**03** passed away

DAY 32

04 pay the piper
動　句　費用を負担する、報いを受ける

It will come the day when you have to pay the piper.
あなたが報いを受けねばならない日が来るだろう。

▶▶ He who pays the piper calls the tune.「費用［責任］を受け持つ者に決定権がある」《諺》

05 pay through the nose
動　句　インフォーマル　法外な代金を払う

My brother would gladly pay through the nose for a conversion on his car.
車の改造のためなら、兄は喜んで法外な代金を払うだろう。

▶▶ 同様の表現に pay an arm and a leg がある。

06 pick-me-up
名　句　元気を回復させるもの

Julia is making spinach and fruit smoothie as lunchtime pick-her-up.
ランチタイムの元気づけの一杯として、ジュリアはほうれん草とフルーツのスムージーを作っている。

▶▶ コーヒーやアルコールなどの飲み物を指すことが多い。

Let's Review

04 It will come the day when you have to
_____.

あなたが報いを受けねばならない日が来るだろう。

05 My brother would gladly _____ for a conversion on his car.

車の改造のためなら、兄は喜んで法外な代金を払うだろう。

06 Julia is making spinach and fruit smoothie as lunchtime
_____.

ランチタイムの元気づけの一杯として、ジュリアはほうれん草とフルーツのスムージーを作っている。

解答 **04** pay the piper **05** pay through the nose **06** pick-her-up

DAY 32

07 pick the brains of
動 句 知恵を借りる、助言をもらう

I have no idea. I was hoping to pick the brains of marketing experts.

どうすればいいか分からない。マーケティングの専門家の知恵を借りられるといいのだが。

▶▶ ちょっとした相談、ちょっとしたアドバイスをもらいたい時に使う。

08 piece of cake
名 スラング とても簡単なこと、朝めし前のこと

Finding the right designer is a piece of cake.

適任のデザイナーを見つけるのはとても簡単だ。

▶▶ 一切れのケーキをペロリと食べるように簡単という意味。

09 piss off
動 スラング 卑 立ち去る

You are irrelevant in my life. Now piss off.

あなたは私の人生とは無関係だ。いますぐ立ち去れ。

▶▶ go away と同義だが、より強く失礼な表現。

Let's Review

07 I have no idea. I was hoping to _____ marketing experts.

どうすればいいか分からない。マーケティングの専門家の知恵を借りられるといいのだが。

08 Finding the right designer is a _____.

適任のデザイナーを見つけるのはとても簡単だ。

09 You are irrelevant in my life. Now _____.

あなたは私の人生とは無関係だ。いますぐ立ち去れ。

解答 **07** pick the brains of   **08** piece of cake   **09** piss off

⑩ play on
[動] 利用する、つけこむ

The underwear salesman played on the woman's wish to look sexy.
下着のセールスマンは、セクシーに見せたいというその女性の願望につけこんだ。

▶▶ on は前置詞で、後ろに目的語をとる。

⑪ play one's cards right
[動][句][インフォーマル] うまくやる、上手に振る舞う

She might be going to the LPGA championship this year, if she plays her cards right.
うまくやれば、彼女は今年LPGAチャンピオンシップに行くかもしれない。

▶▶「トランプ遊びをする」は play (at) cards。

⑫ pour out
[動] 打ち明ける

Julia poured out her troubles to Mark.
ジュリアはマークに自分のトラブルを打ち明けた。

▶▶ give tongue to, utter, verbalize と同義。

Let's Review

10 The underwear salesman _____ the woman's wish to look sexy.

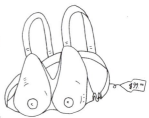

下着のセールスマンは、セクシーに見せたいというその女性の願望につけこんだ。

11 She might be going to the LPGA championship this year, if she _____.

うまくやれば、彼女は今年 LPGA チャンピオンシップに行くかもしれない。

12 Julia _____ her troubles to Mark.

ジュリアはマークに自分のトラブルを打ち明けた。

解答 **10** played on **11** plays her cards right **12** poured out

01 promise the moon

動 句 途方もないことを約束する

You've had a lot of people promise you the moon, but I'll actually get it for you.

あなたは多くの人に途方もない約束をさせたが、私が実際にかなえてあげよう。

▶▶ promise the earth とも言う。

02 pull one's leg

動 句 **インフォーマル** (ふざけて)だます、からかう

My BlackBerry phone knows how to pull my leg for the right moments.

僕の BlackBerry は、いいタイミングで僕をからかう方法を知っているんだ。

▶▶ 単に「からかう」という意味で、そこに「足を引っ張る（他人の行動を妨げる）」というニュアンスはない。

03 pull strings

動 句 **インフォーマル** 陰で糸を引く、手助けするために陰で影響力を行使する

I love when people have connections. They always pull strings for us.

人々がつながっている時が大好きだ。彼らはいつでも陰ながら助けてくれる。

▶▶ 操り人形のイメージから。

Let's Review

01 You've had a lot of people _____, but I'll actually get it for you.

あなたは多くの人に途方もない約束をさせたが、私が実際にかなえてあげよう。

02 My BlackBerry phone knows how to _____ for the right moments.

僕の BlackBerry は、いいタイミングで僕をからかう方法を知っているんだ。

03 I love when people have connections. They always _____ for us.

人々がつながっている時が大好きだ。彼らはいつでも陰ながら助けてくれる。

解答 **01** promise you the moon　**02** pull my leg　**03** pull strings

DAY 33

 ## pushover
名 だまされやすい人、言いなりになる人

Mark can't control Julia, but he is not a pushover no more!

マークはジュリアを支配することはできないが、もはや言いなりではない。

▶▶ いわゆる気が弱い人のことを言う。push over は「席を詰める、押し倒す」。

 ## put up with
動 我慢する

I've been waiting 5 years to meet him, but I'm not gonna put up with all that tomorrow.

私は彼に会うために5年間待ち続けてきたけれど、明日はそんな風に我慢するつもりはない。

▶▶ tolerate と同義、嫌なことを「我慢する、受け入れる」というニュアンス。

 ## put words into one's mouth
動 句 (人が) 言いもしないことを言ったことにする

Please don't put words into my mouth. I never ever said anything like that before.

私がそう言ったなんて言わないでください。これまで一度も、そんなことは決して口にしていません。

▶▶ 自分が言っていないことを言ったことのように思われている誤解を解きたいときなどに使う。

Let's Review

04 Mark can't control Julia, but he is not a _____ no more!

マークはジュリアを支配することはできないが、もはや言いなりではない。

05 I've been waiting 5 years to meet him, but I'm not gonna _____ all that tomorrow.

私は彼に会うために5年間待ち続けてきたけれど、明日はそんな風に我慢するつもりはない。

06 Please don't _____. I never ever said anything like that before.

私がそう言ったなんて言わないでください。これまで一度も、そんなことは決して口にしていません。

解答 **04** pushover **05** put up with **06** put words into my mouth

07 put money where your mouth is

言ったことを行動で見せる

Hey, you gotta put money where your mouth is.

ほら、君は態度で示さなきゃだめだよ。

▶▶ make/take a bet と同義。

08 quite the thing

名 句　当世流行のもの

Female smoking is quite the thing these days.

女性の喫煙が昨今の流行だ。

▶▶ 類義語として modern, contemporary, advanced, state-of-the-art。

09 rain check

名 句　延期

Thanks, but I'll take a rain check. I must get this finished tonight.

ありがとう、でも延期するよ。今夜これを仕上げないといけないんだ。

▶▶ rain check は、野球などスポーツの試合が雨で中止になったときに渡される「雨天順延券」のこと。

Let's Review

07 Hey, you gotta _____.

ほら、君は態度で示さなきゃだめだよ。

08 Female smoking is _____ these days.

女性の喫煙が昨今の流行だ。

09 Thanks, but I'll take a _____. I must get this finished tonight.

ありがとう、でも延期するよ。今夜これを仕上げないといけないんだ。

解答　**07** put money where your mouth is　**08** quite the thing　**09** rain check

DAY 33

 read the riot act
動　句　(親、教師などが)きつく叱る

The journalists should read the riot act.
ジャーナリストたるものは、厳しく糾弾する姿勢を持つべきだ。

▶▶ reprehend と同義。

---

 right on
形　スラング　賛成、頑張れ、いいぞ

You have got to succeed in doing what is necessary; Right on!
君は、必要なことを成功させなければならない。がんばれ！

▶▶ right on target か right on cue のどちらかが短くなった表現と言われている。

---

 ring a bell
動　句　心当たりがある、ピンとくる

I knew your name rang a bell. How have you been? What are you up to these days?
君の名前にピンと来たんだ。元気にしていた？　最近は何をしているの？

▶▶ 特に人の名前に聞き覚えがある、見覚えがあるときの表現。

Let's Review

10 The journalists should _____.

ジャーナリストたるものは、厳しく糾弾する姿勢を持つべきだ。

11 You have got to succeed in doing what is necessary; _____!

君は、必要なことを成功させなければならない。がんばれ！

12 I knew your name _____. How have you been? What are you up to these days?

君の名前にピンと来たんだ。元気にしていた？ 最近は何をしているの？

解答 **10** read the riot act **11** Right on **12** rang a bell

01 rip-off
名 スラング 詐欺、(粗悪・違法な)模造品

Electronic cigarettes are a proven rip-off.
電子たばこは粗悪品であると立証済みだ。

▶▶ 句動詞 rip off の意味は「奪う、だまし取る、法外な料金を要求する」。

---

02 rob the cradle

動 句 インフォーマル はるかに年下の相手と結婚(交際)する

My grandmother recently robbed the cradle.
祖母はこのほど、はるかに年下の相手と結婚した。

▶▶ 反意語は rob the grave「ずっと年上の人と結婚[恋愛]する」。

---

03 roller coaster ride

名 句 激しく変動して

Eva's emotions have taken her on a serious roller coaster ride over the last couple of weeks.
ここ数週間、エヴァの感情は相当激しく上下している。

▶▶ Sturm und Drang, upheaval, turbulence と同義。

Let's Review

01 Electronic cigarettes are a proven _____.

電子たばこは粗悪品であると立証済みだ。

02 My grandmother recently _____.

祖母はこのほど、はるかに年下の相手と結婚した。

03 Eva's emotions have taken her on a serious _____ over the last couple of weeks.

ここ数週間、エヴァの感情は相当激しく上下している。

解答 **01** rip-off　**02** robbed the cradle　**03** roller coaster ride

DAY 34

04 root for
動 句 (熱狂的に)応援する

New York Knicks are the most difficult NBA team to root for.
ニューヨーク・ニックスは、応援するのが最も難しい NBA チームだ。

▶▶ スポーツについて話す時などによく使われる。反意語は side against。

05 rule out
動 排除する、外す

He continues to rule out that option.
彼はその選択肢を外し続けている。

▶▶ ニュースや刑事もののドラマなどでもよく使われる表現。

06 run off
動 句 ❶印刷する

Can I get you to run off 10 copies of these documents?
この書類のコピーを 10 部お願いできますか？

❷逃げる、駆け落ちする

I love this part when she runs off with the chicken!
彼女がニワトリと一緒に逃げるシーンが大好きなの！

▶▶ run off は他にも多くの意味があるので辞書でチェックしておこう。

Let's Review

04 New York Knicks are the most difficult NBA team to _____.

ニューヨーク・ニックスは、応援するのが最も難しい NBA チームだ。

05 He continues to _____ that option.

彼はその選択肢を外し続けている。

06 Can I get you to _____ 10 copies of these documents?

この書類のコピーを 10 部お願いできますか？

解答　**04** root for　**05** rule out　**06** run off

DAY 34

07 run over
動 ❶(人・物を)ひく

My face is like a pizza that got run over by a truck.

私の顔はトラックにひかれたピザみたいだ。

❷見直す、復習する

Julia ran over the book so she would remember them for the test.

テストのために暗記しようと、ジュリアはその本を復習した。

▶▶ run over は他にも多くの意味があるので辞書でチェックしておこう。

08 run that by me again
動 句 インフォーマル もう一度言って[説明して]ください

Wait, let me run that by you again.

待って、もう一度説明させてください。

▶▶ run 〜 by で「(人)に〜を説明する」。

09 save the day
動 句 急場を救う、事なきを得る

I was so starving and this pizza saved the day.

私はとても空腹で、このピザに救われた。

Thanks for saving the day, Iron Man.

アイアンマン、危ないところを助けてくれてありがとう。

▶▶ "You saved the day." は、「あなたのおかげで助かりました」という意味になる。

Let's Review

07 My face is like a pizza that got _____ by a truck.

私の顔はトラックにひかれたピザみたいだ。

08 Wait, let me _____ _____.

待って、もう一度説明させてください。

09 I was so starving and this pizza _____.

私はとても空腹で、このピザに救われた。

解答　**07** run over　**08** run that by me again　**09** saved the day

DAY 34

10 say a mouthful
動 句　インフォーマル　(重要な)ことを言う

Sometimes you can say a mouthful by not saying anything at all.

時には一言も話さないことで、大切なことを伝えられる。

▶▶ "You said a mouthful." は、「あなたの言うとおりだよ」という意味で返答で用いる。

---

11 scratch the surface
動 句　表面しか見ない

If all you do is scratching the surface, it'll take you forever to get to the core.

表面しか見ないと、永遠に核心にたどりつけないよ。

▶▶ 同様の意味で skim the surface という表現もある。

---

12 screw up
動 句　スラング　卑　台無しにする、大失敗する

I screwed up the finals yesterday.

私は昨日、最終試験で大失敗した。

▶▶ この表現は fuck up の婉曲表現だという説がある。

Let's Review

10 Sometimes you can _____ by not saying anything at all.

時には一言も話さないことで、大切なことを伝えられる。

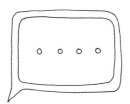

11 If all you do is _____, it'll take you forever to get to the core.

表面しか見ないと、永遠に核心にたどりつけないよ。

12 I _____ the finals yesterday.

私は昨日、最終試験で大失敗した。

解答 **10** say a mouthful **11** scratching the surface **12** screwed up

DAY 35

01 second thought
名 考え直すこと

On second thought I should not watch this movie again. I don't need reminders of sadness.

考え直してみると、私はこの映画をもう一度見るべきではない。悲しみを思い出させるものは必要ないんだ。

▶▶ afterthought, rethink, reconsideration と同義。

02 second wind
名 回復した元気

Julia was going to bed, but she got her second wind and now she is cutting out fun things from magazines to make a bookmark.

ジュリアは寝ようとしていたが、元気を回復した。いまは、しおりを作るために雑誌から面白いところを切り抜いている。

▶▶ 元は、運動後に息切れをしたあとの「回復した呼吸」を意味する語。

03 see things
動 句 インフォーマル 幻を見る

Ophelia told her husband someone had been at the window, but he told her she was seeing things.

オフィーリアは、窓際に誰かがいたと夫に言ったが、彼は妻に見間違いだと言った。

▶▶ see の意味が「自然に目に入ってくる」ことから、「幻のように通常見えないものが見えてしまう」という意味を表す。

Let's Review

01 On _____ I should not watch this movie again. I don't need reminders of sadness.

考え直してみると、私はこの映画をもう一度見るべきではない。悲しみを思い出させるものは必要ないんだ。

02 Julia was going to bed, but she got her _____ and now she is cutting out fun things from magazines to make a bookmark.

ジュリアは寝ようとしていたが、元気を回復した。いまは、しおりを作るために雑誌から面白いところを切り抜いている。

03 Ophelia told her husband someone had been at the window, but he told her she was _____.

オフィーリアは、窓際に誰かがいたと夫に言ったが、彼は妻に見間違いだと言った。

解答 **01** second thought **02** second wind **03** seeing things

DAY 35

04 set out
動 出発する

It is time to set out and watch the ocean.
出発して、海を見に行く時だ。

▶▶ 行き先を示す時は for が続く。

---

05 set the world on fire
動 句 インフォーマル 大成功をおさめる、世間をあっと言わせる

Apple is going to set the world on fire with their smart watch.
Apple は同社のスマートウォッチで、世間をあっと言わせようとしている。

▶▶ set on fire は「火をつける、火を放つ」という意味。

---

06 show off
動 句 見せびらかす

Once, my girlfriend had a car accident showing off her driving skill.
僕のガールフレンドはかつて、運転技術を見せびらかして交通事故を起こした。

▶▶ 持っているもの (体、所有物など) をひけらかす、という意味で使う。

Let's Review

04 It is time to _____ and watch the ocean.

出発して、海を見に行く時だ。

05 Apple is going to _____ with their smart watch.

Apple は同社のスマートウォッチで、世間をあっと言わせようとしている。

06 Once, my girlfriend had a car accident _____ her driving skill.

僕のガールフレンドはかつて、運転技術を見せびらかして交通事故を起こした。

解答 **04** set out **05** set the world on fire **06** showing off

DAY 35

 ## sick and tired
形 〜にまったくうんざりして

Julia has been really missing Mark and she has been so sick and tired of waiting.
ジュリアは本当にマークを恋しがっていて、待つことにまったくうんざりしていた。

▶▶ sick/tired to death とも言う。

 ## sink in
動 インフォーマル 十分に理解される

Hopefully the fact that she is gone will sink in while I sleep.
私が眠っている間に、彼女が去っていったという事実がきちんと理解できるといいのだが。

▶▶ 類義語として get through, get across, dawn, penetrate など。

 ## sleep a wink
動 句 (通常否定形で) 一睡も

I couldn't sleep a wink for some reason. Today is going to be a bad day.
どういうわけか、一睡もできなかった。今日は悪い日になりそうだ。

▶▶ 「まばたきひとつの間だけ眠る」という意味から、何らかの理由で全く眠れないときによく使われる表現。

Let's Review

07 Julia has been really missing Mark and she has been so _____ of waiting.

ジュリアは本当にマークを恋しがっていて、待つことにまったくうんざりしていた。

08 Hopefully the fact that she is gone will _____ while I sleep.

私が眠っている間に、彼女が去っていったという事実がきちんと理解できるといいのだが。

09 I couldn't _____ for some reason. Today is going to be a bad day.

どういうわけか、一睡もできなかった。今日は悪い日になりそうだ。

解答 **07** sick and tired　**08** sink in　**09** sleep a wink

DAY 35

⑩ sleep like a dog
動 句 ぐっすり眠る

Brian is getting ready for bed and hoping to sleep like a dog.
ブライアンは寝る準備もできたし、ぐっすり眠りたいと思っている。

▶▶ working like a dog は「懸命に働く」、die like a dog は「憐れな死に方をする」。

⑪ sleep on
動 ～を一晩寝かせる、～を一晩寝て考える

I will sleep on it and get back to you tomorrow.
一晩考えて、明日お返事します。

▶▶ 文字通り一晩(または何日間か)寝て考えてみるという感じ。

⑫ smell a rat
動 句 インフォーマル うさんくさく思う、変だと感づく

Anyone received a google award email this morning? Somehow I smelled a rat and not open it.
今朝、グーグル賞のEメールを受け取った人はいる？ どうもうさんくさくて、僕は開いていない。

▶▶ 同様の意味では他に smell fishy, shady, (be) off などがある。

Let's Review

10 Brian is getting ready for bed and hoping to _____.

ブライアンは寝る準備もできたし、ぐっすり眠りたいと思っている。

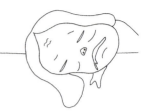

11 I will _____ it and get back to you tomorrow.

一晩考えて、明日お返事します。

12 Anyone received a google award email this morning? Somehow I _____ and not open it.

今朝、グーグル賞のEメールを受け取った人はいる？ どうもうさんくさくて、僕は開いていない。

解答 **10** sleep like a dog **11** sleep on **12** smelled a rat

DAY 36

01 so far, so good
インフォーマル これまでは順調である

This is his first week of being General Manager. So far, so good.

今週は、ゼネラルマネージャーとしての彼の最初の週だ。これまでのところは順調だ。

▶▶ まだ完了していないことに対して使う。

02 speak of the devil and he appears
ことわざ うわさをすれば影

I guess it's true speak of the devil and he appears.

うわさをすれば影というのは本当だと思うよ。

▶▶ うわさをしていた相手が現れたときに使う表現。

03 split hairs
動 句 (ささいなことに)こだわる

Julia is always splitting hairs; she often starts an argument about something small.

ジュリアはいつも細かいことにこだわる。小さなことについて、たびたび議論を始める。

▶▶ hairsplitter「重箱の隅をつつく人」、hairsplitting「重箱の隅をつつくような」といった派生語がある。

Let's Review

01 This is his first week of being General Manager.

_____.

今週は、ゼネラルマネージャーとしての彼の最初の週だ。これまでのところは順調だ。

02 I guess it's true

_____.

うわさをすれば影というのは本当だと思うよ。

03 Julia is always _____; she often starts an argument about something small.

ジュリアはいつも細かいことにこだわる。小さなことについて、たびたび議論を始める。

解答 **01** So far, so good **02** speak of the devil and he appears
03 splitting hairs

DAY 36

04 spring chicken
名 スラング ひよっ子

Ophelia lives life to the full. She is no spring chicken.
オフィーリアは存分に人生を生きている。彼女はもうひよっ子なんかではない。

▶▶ 否定形の no spring chicken「もう子どもでは［若くは］ない」は主に女性に対して用いられる。

---

05 stab in the back
動 句 スラング 裏切る

I'm only 20 years old but I know what's being stabbed in the back by my friends.
僕はまだ 20 歳だが、友達に裏切られるのがどんなことか知っている。

▶▶ stab in the wallet だと「手痛い出費」、stab in the dark は「当て推量」。

---

06 stand in for
動 句 スラング 代理を務める

Brian will stand in for Mark while he is away.
マークが留守の間、ブライアンが代理を務める。

▶▶ be a substitute for, cover for, take the place of と同義。

Let's Review

04 Ophelia lives life to the full. She is no _____.

オフィーリアは存分に人生を生きている。彼女はもうひよっ子なんかではない。

05 I'm only 20 years old but I know what's being _____ by my friends.

僕はまだ20歳だが、友達に裏切られるのがどんなことか知っている。

06 Brian will _____ Mark while he is away.

マークが留守の間、ブライアンが代理を務める。

解答 **04** spring chicken   **05** stabbed in the back   **06** stand in for

DAY 36

steal the show
動 句　人気を独占する

Pro basketball player Michael Jordan, is going to steal the show at the upcoming NBA Draft.
プロバスケットボール選手のマイケル・ジョーダンは、来たる NBA のドラフトで人気を独占するだろう。

▶▶ steal the spotlight とも言う。

---

stick-in-the-mud
名　インフォーマル　保守的な、頭の固い、のろま

Stop being a stick-in-the-mud and get out there and have fun.
堅苦しいのは止めて、そこから出てきて楽しみなさい。

Julia is a bit of a stick-in-the-mud.
ジュリアはちょっとのろまだね。

▶▶ 泥の中に刺さった小枝を動かそうとしてもほとんど動かない様子から。

---

stuck on
形　スラング　〜に夢中である

Brian is stuck on Ophelia.
ブライアンはオフィーリアに夢中だ。

▶▶ 「(問題など)が解けずに行き詰まる」という意味もある。

Let's Review

07 Pro basketball player Michael Jordan, is going to _____ at the upcoming NBA Draft.

プロバスケットボール選手のマイケル・ジョーダンは、来たる NBA のドラフトで人気を独占するだろう。

08 Stop being a _____ and get out there and have fun.

堅苦しいのは止めて、そこから出てきて楽しみなさい。

09 Brian is _____ Ophelia.

ブライアンはオフィーリアに夢中だ。

解答 **07** steal the show **08** stick-in-the-mud **09** stuck on

⑩ sure thing
名 インフォーマル いいとも

"Can you give me a hand with this?" "Sure thing."
「これを手伝ってくれる？」「いいとも」

▶▶ 何かをしてあげた相手から Thank you. などとお礼を言われたときに、その返答として Sure thing. と言うこともある。

⑪ swallow one's words
動 句 自分の過ちを認める，前言を取り消す

I'm gonna succeed and watch you swallow your words back.
僕はきっと成功して，君が前言を取り消すのを見るつもりだよ。

▶▶ eat one's words と同義。

⑫ take advantage of
動 句 利用する

Companies can make money by taking advantage of the growing financial power of women. Investors should consider buying retail stocks.
企業は、増大している女性の経済力を利用して金を稼ぐことができる。投資家たちは小売株の購入を検討すべきだ。

▶▶ 比較的悪い内容で用いる場合が多い。

Let's Review

10 "Can you give me a hand with this?" "_____."

「これを手伝ってくれる？」「いいとも」

11 I'm gonna succeed and watch you _____ back.

僕はきっと成功して，君が前言を取り消すのを見るつもりだよ。

12 Companies can make money by _____ the growing financial power of women. Investors should consider buying retail stocks.

企業は、増大している女性の経済力を利用して金を稼ぐことができる。投資家たちは小売株の購入を検討すべきだ。

解答 **10** Sure thing **11** swallow your words **12** taking advantage of

DAY 37

01 take a stand
動句 断固とした態度をとる

It is time for Korean society to take a stand against crime.

韓国社会はそろそろ、犯罪に対して断固とした態度をとる時期だ。

▶▶ 前置詞 for がつくと「賛成」、against だと「反対」の態度をとる意味になる。

02 take back
動 撤回する

Shall I take back everything I've ever said?

いままでの発言をすべて撤回しましょうか？

▶▶ 似た表現に back down「(言ったこと、主張を) 取り消す」がある。

03 take it on the chin
動句 インフォーマル 耐え忍ぶ

No matter what life throws at me, I stay positive and take it on the chin. I know no other way.

人生が何を投げかけてこようとも、私は前向きさを忘れずに耐え忍ぶ。ほかに方法はないとわかっているのだ。

▶▶ ボクシングで、パンチをあごに食らうところから。take it on the nose と同義。

Let's Review

01 It is time for Korean society to _____ against crime.

韓国社会はそろそろ、犯罪に対して断固とした態度をとる時期だ。

02 Shall I _____ everything I've ever said?

いままでの発言をすべて撤回しましょうか？

03 No matter what life throws at me, I stay positive and _____. I know no other way.

人生が何を投げかけてこようとも、私は前向きさを忘れずに耐え忍ぶ。ほかに方法はないとわかっているのだ。

解答 **01** take a stand　**02** take back　**03** take it on the chin

DAY 37

04 taken aback
形 びっくりした

Julia was taken aback when the bus driver greeted just as she entered the bus. Good to know good-mannered people still exist.

バスに乗り込んだ途端に運転手があいさつをしたので、ジュリアはびっくりした。礼儀正しい人がまだいるのだとわかるとうれしいものだ。

▶▶ aback「後方へ」がベースになった表現だが、単語 aback そのものは現代英語では使われない。

05 take the edge off
動 句 和らげる、弱める

Eva is learning yoga to take the edge off her stress.

エヴァはストレスを和らげるためにヨガを習っている。

▶▶ 「(刃物の)刃をなまらせる」から。

06 talk back
動 インフォーマル 口答えをする

Don't you ever talk back to your daddy!

二度と父に口答えをするな!

▶▶ 親や年上、または目上の人に対して言い返すときに使う。

Let's Review

04 Julia was _____ when the bus driver greeted just as she entered the bus. Good to know good-mannered people still exist.

バスに乗り込んだ途端に運転手があいさつをしたので、ジュリアはびっくりした。礼儀正しい人がまだいるのだとわかるとうれしいものだ。

05 Eva is learning yoga to _____ her stress.

エヴァはストレスを和らげるためにヨガを習っている。

06 Don't you ever _____ to your daddy!

二度と父に口答えをするな！

解答 **04** taken aback **05** take the edge off **06** talk back

07 **taper down**
形 句 だんだんと減る、次第に細くなっていく

Eva has tapered down her smoking to five cigarettes a day.

エヴァはだんだんと喫煙量を減らして、1日5本とした。

▶▶ "taper off" は完全になくなるまで（徐々に減っていく）というニュアンスがあるが、"taper down" にはそこまでの意味はない。

08 **tell on**
動 ～のことを告げ口する

Please don't tell on me no more.

これ以上、私のことを告げ口しないでください。

▶▶ 1539年英訳版の聖書サムエル記上第27章11節より。"David saved neither man nor woman ... for fear (said he) lest they should tell on us."

09 **the creeps**
名 インフォーマル ぞっとする感じ

Guitar and drums on Metallica's songs are still giving me the creeps.

メタリカの曲のギターとドラムを聞くと、いまだにぞっとする。

▶▶ the willies と同義。チャールズ・ディケンズ『デイヴィッド・コパフィールド』で登場人物が自分の病状を "the creeps" と呼んだのから転じて。

Let's Review

07 Eva has _____ her smoking to five cigarettes a day.

エヴァはだんだんと喫煙量を減らして、1日5本とした。

08 Please don't _____ me no more.

これ以上、私のことを告げ口しないでください。

09 Guitar and drums on Metallica's songs are still giving me _____.

メタリカの曲のギターとドラムを聞くと、いまだにぞっとする。

解答 **07** tapered down **08** tell on **09** the creeps

DAY 37

⑩ the score
名 スラング 実情

Very few people know the score in the company.
その会社の実情を知っている者はごくわずかしかいない。

▶▶ even/settle the score は「(人)に仕返しをする」。

---

⑪ think aloud
動 (思わず)ひとりごとを言う

A true friend is someone before whom I can think aloud —without comment or criticism.
真の友人とは、その人の目の前で知らず知らずひとりごとを言えるような人だ。意見や批判を入れずに。

▶▶ think out loud とも言う。

---

⑫ think better of
動 見直す、気を変える

I first thought I wasn't impressed but really it is amazing over here when I think better of what I've just seen.
最初は特に気に留めなかったが、自分が目にしたばかりのものを見直してみると、こちらはまさに驚きである。

▶▶「よりよいことを考える」から連想すると覚えやすい。

Let's Review

10 Very few people know _____ in the company.

その会社の実情を知っている者はごくわずかしかいない。

11 A true friend is someone before whom I can _____ —without comment or criticism.

真の友人とは、その人の目の前で知らず知らずひとりごとを言えるような人だ。意見や批判を入れずに。

12 I first thought I wasn't impressed but really it is amazing over here when I _____ what I've just seen.

最初は特に気に留めなかったが、自分が目にしたばかりのものを見直してみると、こちらはまさに驚きである。

解答 **10** the score **11** think aloud **12** think better of

01 think over
動 熟考する、考え直す

If you don't mind, I'd like some time to think it over.
もしよろしければ、それについて熟考する時間をいただきたいと思います。

▶▶ 副詞 over には「もう一度」という意味がある。

02 through the grapevine
副句 うわさで耳にする

I've heard through the grapevine that Alice had been dating Brian for almost a year.
アリスがブライアンと1年近くつきあっていると、うわさで耳にした。

▶▶ 南北戦争時代、ニューヨークの Grapevine という酒場にスパイや政治家たちが集まって噂やゴシップを広めていたのが語源の一つと言われている。

03 through thick and thin
副句 よい時も悪い時も、終始変わらずに

Jobs needs a partner that is going to stick with him through thick and thin.
ジョブズは、よい時も悪い時も一緒にいてくれるパートナーを必要としている。

▶▶ 元の表現は through thicket and thin wood。昔、英国が森林に覆われていた時代、人は旅を急ぐ時に道のない森の中を通ったことから。

Let's Review

01 If you don't mind, I'd like some time to _____.

もしよろしければ、それについて熟考する時間をいただきたいと思います。

02 I've heard _____ that Alice had been dating Brian for almost a year.

アリスがブライアンと1年近くつきあっていると、うわさで耳にした。

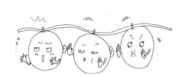

03 Jobs needs a partner that is going to stick with him _____.

ジョブズは、よい時も悪い時も一緒にいてくれるパートナーを必要としている。

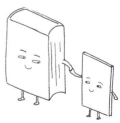

解答 **01** think it over　**02** through the grapevine　**03** through thick and thin

DAY 38

throw in the towel
動句 インフォーマル 敗北を認める、降参する

I'm still amazed at how fast HP threw in the towel on their touchpad tablet.

タッチパッドタブレットでの敗北を HP がこんなに早く認めたことに、私はいまだに驚いている。

▶▶ ボクシングで試合放棄しなければならないとき、敗北を認めるしるしにセコンドがリングにタオルを投げ入れることから。

tickle pink
動句 インフォーマル 抱腹絶倒させる

Is there someone who can accept my flaws, forgive my mistakes, and tickle me pink until I can't breathe?

私の欠点を受け入れ、失敗を許し、息ができなくなるまで笑わせてくれる人はいないかな？

▶▶ pink である理由は、人は嬉しくなると顔色がピンクになるからだ、という説がある。

tie the knot
動句 インフォーマル 結婚する

Jolie and Pitt have just tied the knot.

ジョリーとピットは結婚したばかりだ。

▶▶ 「結び目を作る」ことから結婚するという意味になった。

Let's Review

04 I'm still amazed at how fast HP _____ on their touchpad tablet.

タッチパッドタブレットでの敗北を HP がこんなに早く認めたことに、私はいまだに驚いている。

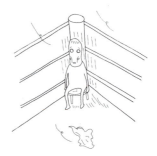

05 Is there someone who can accept my flaws, forgive my mistakes, and _____ until I can't breathe?

私の欠点を受け入れ、失敗を許し、息ができなくなるまで笑わせてくれる人はいないかな？

06 Jolie and Pitt have just _____.

ジョリーとピットは結婚したばかりだ。

解答　**04** threw in the towel　**05** tickle me pink　**06** tied the knot

DAY 38

07 tighten one's belt
動 句 倹約する、出費を抑える

Due to financial pressure from the increased cost of living, I've got to tighten my belt.
生活費が増大して家計が圧迫されているので、倹約しなければならない。

 十分に食べるものがなく、ベルトをきつく締めたことから「倹約する、耐乏生活をする」という意味でも使われる。

08 time and again
副 繰り返し

Time and again, nature shows that there is more than one right answer.
正しい答えはひとつだけではないということを、自然は繰り返し証明している。

 again and again, over and over と同義。

09 tip the scales
動 句 インフォーマル 有利に働く、形勢を一変させる

Beautiful presentation can tip the scales in your favor.
見事なプレゼンテーションは、あなたに有利に働くだろう。

 tilt/turn the scale(s) とも言う。

Let's Review

07 Due to financial pressure from the increased cost of living, I've got to _____.

生活費が増大して家計が圧迫されているので、倹約しなければならない。

08 _____, nature shows that there is more than one right answer.

正しい答えはひとつだけではないということを、自然は繰り返し証明している。

09 Beautiful presentation can _____ in your favor.

見事なプレゼンテーションは、あなたに有利に働くだろう。

解答　07 tighten my belt　08 Time and again　09 tip the scales

DAY 38

⑩ to a man
副 句 一人残らず、満場一致で

The workers voted to a man to go on a strike.

労働者たちは、一人残らずストライキ実施に投票した。

▶▶ man は "everyone" の意味。最近まれに、女性だけのグループを表す時 "to a woman" が使われることもある。

---

⑪ to a turn
副 句 ちょうどよく、適度に

My steak has been done to a turn.

私のステーキは焼き加減がちょうどよかった。

▶▶ 肉の焼き具合など、主に料理で使用される。

---

⑫ to boot
副 句 おまけに、その上

Ophelia is tall, beautiful, and friendly to boot.

オフィーリアは長身で美しく、おまけに親切だ。

▶▶ この boot は靴のことではなく、advantage などを意味する古英語 bōt、または中英語 bōte が元になっている。

Let's Review

10 The workers voted _____ to go on a strike.

労働者たちは、一人残らずストライキ実施に投票した。

VOTE PERCENTAGE

11 My steak has been done _____.

私のステーキは焼き加減がちょうどよかった。

12 Ophelia is tall, beautiful, and friendly _____.

オフィーリアは長身で美しく、おまけに親切だ。

解答 **10** to a man **11** to a turn **12** to boot

01 top-drawer
形 インフォーマル 最上級の、最高の

Messi's that last goal from yesterday's match. Top-drawer.
昨日の試合での、メッシのあのラストゴール。最高だったよ。

▶▶ ビクトリア朝時代の貴族が、寝室の整理ダンスの一番上の引き出しに、宝石や最高級の服など最も高価なものをしまっていたことから。

02 to speak of
形 句 インフォーマル とりたてて言うほどの,注目に値するほどの

Alice has got no friends to speak of.
アリスにはとりたてて言うほどの友達は一人もいなかった。

No more incidents in Seoul to speak of. Police and Community Safety Patrols are still on duty doing fantastic work.
ソウルには注目に値するほどの事件はもはや存在しない。警察や地域安全パトロール隊がいまも任務に当たり、素晴らしい働きをしているのだ。

▶▶ 通例、否定文で用いられる。

03 to this day
副 句 いまでも、今日に至るまで

The spirit of the revolution continues to this day.
革命の精神はいまも息づいている。

▶▶ 過去のことが今でも続いている状態を表す際に「今日に至るまで」や「現在でも」などの意味として用いる。

Let's Review

01 Messi's that last goal from yesterday's match. _____.

昨日の試合での、メッシのあのラストゴール。最高だったよ。

02 Alice has got no friends _____.

アリスにはとりたてて言うほどの友達は一人もいなかった。

03 The spirit of the revolution continues _____.

革命の精神はいまも息づいている。

解答 **01** Top-drawer　**02** to speak of　**03** to this day

DAY 39

 trial and error

名 試行錯誤、トライアル・アンド・エラー

Children strive because of curiosity. But that's all apart of developmental growth. Trial and error.

子どもが一生懸命に努力するのは好奇心があるからだ。しかし、それもすべて発達段階の一部である。試行錯誤しているのだ。

▶▶ 技術分野では cut and try とも言う。

 try one's hand

動 句 (初めて)〜をやってみる

Eva decided to try her hand at painting today.

エヴァは、今日は水彩画をやってみようと決めた。

▶▶ 前置詞 at を伴うことが多い。

 turn the tide

動 句 流れを変える、形勢を一変させる

Michael Jordan's coming turned the tide for Chicago Bulls, and the Bulls won.

マイケル・ジョーダンが入るとシカゴブルズの流れが変わり、ブルズは勝利した。

▶▶ 状況や意見、プロセスが大きく変わったときなどに使う。

Let's Review

04 Children strive because of curiosity. But that's all apart of developmental growth.

_____.

子どもが一生懸命に努力するのは好奇心があるからだ。しかし、それもすべて発達段階の一部である。試行錯誤しているのだ。

05 Eva decided to _____ at painting today.

エヴァは、今日は水彩画をやってみようと決めた。

06 Michael Jordan's coming _____ for Chicago Bulls, and the Bulls won.

マイケル・ジョーダンが入るとシカゴブルズの流れが変わり、ブルズは勝利した。

解答　**04** Trial and error　**05** try her hand　**06** turned the tide

DAY 39

07 twiddle one's thumbs
動 句 (両手の指を4本ずつ組んで)親指をくるくる回す(退屈しているしぐさ)、(何もしないで)のらくらしている

Mark will wait at home to twiddle his thumbs until the new iPhone comes.

マークはすることもなく、ただ新しい iPhone が届くのを家で待つだろう。

▶▶ 何もしていないときに、ぼんやりと両手の指を組んで互いの親指を回すしぐさから。

08 two-time
動 スラング (恋人・配偶者を)裏切る,浮気をする

She cried when she found that her boyfriend was two-timing her.

ボーイフレンドが浮気をしているとわかると、彼女は泣き叫んだ。

▶▶ cheat と同義。

09 under a cloud
形 句 疑われて

Eva's roommate was kept under a cloud of suspicion.

エヴァのルームメイトは疑いをかけられていた。

▶▶ 疑わしい相手の頭の上に黒雲が立ち込めているようなイメージ。

Let's Review

07 Mark will wait at home to _____ until the new iPhone comes.

マークはすることもなく，ただ新しいiPhone が届くのを家で待つだろう。

08 She cried when she found that her boyfriend was _____ her.

ボーイフレンドが浮気をしているとわかると，彼女は泣き叫んだ。

09 Eva's roommate was kept _____ of suspicion.

エヴァのルームメイトは疑いをかけられていた。

解答 **07** twiddle his thumbs **08** two-timing **09** under a cloud

DAY 39

 under one's breath

副 句 声を潜めて、小声で

Mark heard Eva said something under her breath and he asked her to repeat it aloud.

エヴァが小声で何か言ったのを耳にして、マークは大きな声でもう一度言ってくれと彼女に頼んだ。

▶▶ sotto voce と同義。

 under one's wing

副 句 (人)の面倒をみる、保護する

I feel like I should take these young men under my wings, teach them how to be gentlemen and how to treat women right.

この若い男たちの面倒をみて、紳士的なふるまいや女性に対する正しい接し方を教えるべきではないかと私は思う。

▶▶ 《take + 人 –》特に、自分より若かったり経験の少ない相手を助けたり守るという意味で使用する。

 under the sun

形 副 句 地上の、この世で

Vidal is the best hairdresser ever and he has no rival under the sun.

ヴィダルは史上最高の美容師であり、この世にライバルは一人もいない。

▶▶ 北朝鮮の日常を描いたロシアのドキュメンタリー映画『太陽の下、V luchakh solnca / Under the Sun (2015 年)』は波紋を呼んだ。

Let's Review

10 Mark heard Eva said something _____ and he asked her to repeat it aloud.

エヴァが小声で何か言ったのを耳にして、マークは大きな声でもう一度言ってくれと彼女に頼んだ。

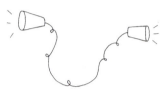

11 I feel like I should take these young men _____, teach them how to be gentlemen and how to treat women right.

この若い男たちの面倒をみて、紳士的なふるまいや女性に対する正しい接し方を教えるべきではないかと私は思う。

12 Vidal is the best hairdresser ever and he has no rival _____.

ヴィダルは史上最高の美容師であり、この世にライバルは一人もいない。

解答 **10** under her breath **11** under my wings **12** under the sun

01 up-and-coming

形　句　前途有望な、成功しそうな

You are all up-and-coming young people who will lead the world into happiness.
君たちはみな、世界を幸福へと導いていくであろう前途有望な若者だ。

▶▶ up は「上昇」、coming は「目標に向かって進んでいる」の意味。

02 ups and downs

名　句　浮き沈み

Life is always about ups and downs. You won't always be at the top, but you won't always be at the bottom either.
人生には常に浮き沈みがあるものだ。常に頂点にいることはないが、常に底辺にいることもない。

▶▶ 同様の表現に ebb and flow がある。

03 uptight

形　スラング　堅苦しい，改まった

I love people with great sense of humor. People these days are too uptight.
私は素晴らしいユーモアセンスのある人が大好きだ。最近の人は堅苦しすぎる。

▶▶ 《be ～》 uptight about で「～について神経質である」。

Let's Review

01 You are all _____ young people who will lead the world into happiness.

君たちはみな、世界を幸福へと導いていくであろう前途有望な若者だ。

02 Life is always about _____. You won't always be at the top, but you won't always be at the bottom either.

人生には常に浮き沈みがあるものだ。常に頂点にいることはないが、常に底辺にいることもない。

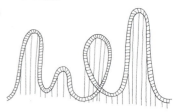

03 I love people with great sense of humor. People these days are too _____.

私は素晴らしいユーモアセンスのある人が大好きだ。最近の人は堅苦しすぎる。

解答 **01** up-and-coming　**02** ups and downs　**03** uptight

DAY 40

use up
動 句 使い切る

Julia cried for almost the whole movie. She used up almost 3 bloody packs of tissue.

ジュリアは、映画の間中ほとんどずっと泣いていた。ティッシュを3箱近くも使い切ってしまった。

▶▶ 「(人を)疲れ果てさせる」という意味もある。

verbal diarrhea
名 句 おしゃべり、病的多弁症

Gust is a nice guy but he's got verbal diarrhea and he can't shut up for a single minute.

ガストはいいやつだがおしゃべりで、1分と黙っていられない。

▶▶ verbosity, logorrhea《医》と同義。

wade in
動 インフォーマル 勢いよく始める、意気込んで加わる

Julia waded in to get the ball from this kid. He threw it to the other kid.

ジュリアはその子からボールを奪おうと意気込んで加わったが、彼は別の子にボールを投げた。

▶▶ 「何らかの動作を開始するために水に入る」という意味から転じて。

Let's Review

04 Julia cried for almost the whole movie. She _____ almost 3 bloody packs of tissue.

ジュリアは、映画の間中ほとんどずっと泣いていた。ティッシュを3箱近くも使い切ってしまった。

05 Gust is a nice guy but he's got _____ and he can't shut up for a single minute.

ガストはいいやつだがおしゃべりで、1分と黙っていられない。

06 Julia _____ to get the ball from this kid. He threw it to the other kid.

ジュリアはその子からボールを奪おうと意気込んで加わったが、彼は別の子にボールを投げた。

解答　04 used up　05 verbal diarrhea　06 waded in

DAY 40

07 wait up
動 句 (人を)寝ずに待つ

Alice's mom was waiting up for her to come home. So sweet!
アリスのママは、彼女が家に帰ってくるのを寝ずに待っていたんだって。優しい人だね!

▶▶ stay awake/up, keep vigil と同義。

---

08 walk in the park
名 句 簡単なもの、容易なこと

Marriage is not like a walk in the park.
結婚は簡単なものではない。

▶▶ walk on eggshells になると「非常に慎重になる、非常に注意深くなる」という意味になる。

---

09 warm up
動 温め直す、ウォーミングアップをする

Ophelia had to warm the sandwich up for dinner.
オフィーリアは夕食用にサンドイッチを温め直さなければならなかった。

Method Man has to warm up his voice before he does the rap – Bring The Pain.
メソッド・マンはラップの『ブリング・ザ・ペイン』を歌う前に、声のウォーミングアップをする必要がある。

▶▶ warm up to + 人で「(人)と打ち解ける」。

Let's Review

07 Alice's mom was _____ for her to come home. So sweet!

アリスのママは、彼女が家に帰ってくるのを寝ずに待っていたんだって。優しい人だね！

08 Marriage is not like a _____.

結婚は簡単なものではない。

09 Ophelia had to _____ the sandwich _____ for dinner.

オフィーリアは夕食用にサンドイッチを温め直さなければならなかった。

解答　**07** waiting up　**08** walk in the park　**09** warm up

DAY 40

waste one's breath
動 句 言葉を無駄に費やす

I barely say 'I love you' anymore. Why waste my breath when most people don't know its meaning.

私はもうめったに「愛している」とは言わない。大半の人がその意味を知らないのに、なぜ私の言葉を無駄に費やすのか。

▶▶ save one's breath は「余計なことは言わない、黙っている」。

way to go
形 句 インフォーマル （人を激励して）いいぞ、その調子だ

Looks like all the positive thoughts paid off. Way to go Brian!

ポジティブな考えがすべて功を奏したようだ。いいぞ、ブライアン！

▶▶ 本来はスポーツでよいプレーをした選手に対するかけ声とし使われていたもの。

weasel word
名 インフォーマル （逃げ口上に使う）あいまいな言葉

Mark is very good at using weasel words to disguise his mind.

マークは、あいまいな言葉を使って自分の気持ちを隠すのが非常にうまい。

▶▶ 通例複数形で使われる。イタチ（weasel）が、卵の中身を吸ったあとに何事もなかったかのように見せかける習性があると考えられていたことより。

Let's Review

10 I barely say 'I love you' anymore. Why _____ when most people don't know its meaning.

私はもうめったに「愛している」とは言わない。大半の人がその意味を知らないのに、なぜ私の言葉を無駄に費やすのか。

11 Looks like all the positive thoughts paid off. _____ Brian!

ポジティブな考えがすべて功を奏したようだ。いいぞ、ブライアン！

12 Mark is very good at using _____ to disguise his mind.

マークは、あいまいな言葉を使って自分の気持ちを隠すのが非常にうまい。

解答　**10** waste my breath　**11** Way to go　**12** weasel words

DAY 41

01 whipping boy
名 句 （他人の失敗などの責任を背負う）身代わり

I used to be the whipping boy during my early days at the company.

会社に入ったばかりのころは、よく身代わりになっていたものだ。

▶▶ 王子と一般市民の子どもを同じ学校で教育する習慣があったころ、悪いことをした王子を罰するわけにはいかず、身代わりの子を罰したことから。

02 white lie
名 句 （人の気持ちを傷つけないための）善意のうそ

I'm all for honesty, but that's the time when a white lie is so much better.

私は誠実さを大切にしているが、いまは善意のうそをつくほうがずっといい時だ。

▶▶ このフレーズで使われている white は harmless（悪意のない）という意味。

03 wise up to
動 句 スラング 気づく

Mark immediately quit his job when he wised up to what was really going on.

マークは、実際に起こっていることに気づくとすぐに仕事を辞めた。

▶▶ wise には形容詞の「賢い」だけでなく動詞で「〜を知る」という意味もある。

Let's Review

01 I used to be the _____ during my early days at the company.

会社に入ったばかりのころは、よく身代わりになっていたものだ。

02 I'm all for honesty, but that's the time when a _____ is so much better.

私は誠実さを大切にしているが、いまは善意のうそをつくほうがずっといい時だ。

03 Mark immediately quit his job when he _____ what was really going on.

マークは、実際に起こっていることに気づくとすぐに仕事を辞めた。

解答 01 whipping boy　02 white lie　03 wised up to

DAY 41

04 word for word
副 句 一語ずつ、文字通りに

This song is describing my life word for word.
この歌は私の人生を文字通りに表現している。

▶▶ exact, verbatim と同義。

---

05 world is one's oyster
前途洋々だ，自由になんでもできる

Mark got up in the morning and he really did feel that the world was his oyster and he started it that way.
マークは朝目が覚めると、自由になんでもできると心から感じ、そんなふうに1日を始めた。

The world is not your oyster.
この世は君の思い通りにはならないよ。

▶▶ シェイクスピア『ウィンザーの陽気な女房たち(The Merry Wives of Windsor)』のセリフのひとつより。

---

06 wrapped up in
形 句 〜に夢中になる

I almost forgot how it was to be 'me' cause I was so wrapped up in him.
私はすっかり彼に夢中になっていたので、「自分」がどんな人間だったかほとんど忘れてしまった。

▶▶ wrapped up は形容詞的表現で「〜で忙しい」となる。wrapped up with a customer「お客様で忙しい」。

Let's Review

04 This song is describing my life _____.

この歌は私の人生を文字通りに表現している。

05 Mark got up in the morning and he really did feel that the _____ and he started it that way.

マークは朝目が覚めると、自由になんでもできると心から感じ、そんなふうに1日を始めた。

06 I almost forgot how it was to be 'me' cause I was so _____ him.

私はすっかり彼に夢中になっていたので、「自分」がどんな人間だったかほとんど忘れてしまった。

解答 **04** word for word **05** world was his oyster **06** wrapped up in

DAY 41

07 write home about
動 句 大したものだ、取りたてて言う

Mark's paintings are nothing to write home about.

マークの絵は大したものではない。

 例文のように、nothing to ～がつくと「話にならない、大したことではない」という意味になる

---

08 X-rated
形 スラング わいせつな、ポルノの

What is the most successful X-rated movie of all time?

いままでで一番成功したポルノ映画は何ですか？

 米国で MPAA（米国映画協会）が指定した film rating（映画観覧制限表示）の X 指定（17 歳未満入場禁止、1991 年廃止）より。

---

09 yes-man
名 インフォーマル イエスマン（目上の人の言うことになんでも賛成する人）

People need to be honest with everyone. If something is wack, tell them. Don't be a yes-man.

人は誰に対しても誠実でなければならない。何かおかしいことがあればそのように伝えなさい。イエスマンになってはいけない。

 brownnoser, stooge, flunky と同義。

Let's Review

07 Mark's paintings are nothing to _____.

マークの絵は大したものではない。

08 What is the most successful _____ movie of all time?

いままでで一番成功したポルノ映画は何ですか？

09 People need to be honest with everyone. If something is wack, tell them. Don't be a _____.

人は誰に対しても誠実でなければならない。何かおかしいことがあればそのように伝えなさい。イエスマンになってはいけない。

解答　**07** write home about　**08** X-rated　**09** yes-man

DAY 41

⑩ you bet
インフォーマル 間違いない

You bet, HumanKind's campaigns will set the world on fire.
間違いない、HumanKind のキャンペーンは大成功を収めるよ。

▶▶ You can bet money on that.「あなたがお金を掛けても確実だよ」という意味より。

---

⑪ your guess is as good as mine
（あなたと同様）私にもよくわからない

"Who will be the next president of Korea?" "I know whom I would prefer, but your guess is as good as mine."
「韓国の次の大統領になるのは誰だろうか？」「好ましい人は知っているのだが、あなたと同様、私にもよくわからないんだ」

▶▶ 通例、質問を受けたときの返答として用いる。

---

⑫ zonk out
動 句 スラング 疲れ果てて眠る，気を失う

Mark was well rested on Friday. Julia said he was zonked out for almost 12 hours straight.
マークは金曜日に十分に休養を取った。約12時間ぶっ通しで眠っていたと、ジュリアが言っていた。

▶▶ zonk は元は強い衝撃音を表す擬声語で、スペルは conk「意識を失う」からきていると言われている。

Let's Review

10 _____, HumanKind's campaigns will set the world on fire.

間違いない、HumanKind のキャンペーンは大成功を収めるよ。

11 "Who will be the next president of Korea?" "I know whom I would prefer, but _____."

「韓国の次の大統領になるのは誰だろうか？」「好ましい人は知っているのだが、あなたと同様、私にもよくわからないんだ」

12 Mark was well rested on Friday. Julia said he was _____ for almost 12 hours straight.

マークは金曜日に十分に休養を取った。約12時間ぶっ通しで眠っていたと、ジュリアが言っていた。

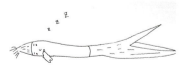

解答　**10** You bet　**11** your guess is as good as mine　**12** zonked out

カバーデザイン　岩目地秀樹（コムデザイン）
イラスト　キム・ボミ
翻　　訳　久松　紀子

スピーキングのための英熟語

2016年 11月7日　第1刷発行

著　者　Matthew D. Kim

発行者　浦　　晋　亮

発行所　IBCパブリッシング株式会社
〒162-0804 東京都新宿区中里町29番3号 菱秀神楽坂ビル9F
Tel. 03-3513-4511　Fax. 03-3513-4512
www.ibcpub.co.jp

印刷所　株式会社シナノパブリッシングプレス

© 2015 Matthew D. Kim
© 2016 IBC Publishing

Printed in Japan

落丁本・乱丁本は、小社宛にお送りください。送料小社負担にてお取り替えいたします。
本書の無断複写(コピー)は著作権法上での例外を除き禁じられています。

ISBN978-4-7946-0444-6